Earl Storey

D1646190

Traditional Roots

TOWARDS AN APPROPRIATE RELATIONSHIP
BETWEEN THE CHURCH OF IRELAND
AND THE ORANGE ORDER

the columba press

First published in 2002 by
the columba press
55A Spruce Avenue, Stillorgan Industrial Park,
Blackrock, Co Dublin

Cover by Bill Bolger
Origination by The Columba Press
Printed in Ireland by ColourBooks Ltd, Dublin

ISBN 1 85607 364 5

Acknowledgements
The author gratefully acknowledges the financial assistance of The
Joseph Rowntree Charitable Trust and of the Community Relations
Council in the research from which this book is derived.

This book has received support from the Northern Ireland Community
Relations Council; promoting a pluralist society characterised by equity,
respect for diversity and interdependence. The views expressed do not
necessarily reflect those of the Community Relations Council.

Contents

Introduction

I can claim a reasonable degree of experience of the Orange Order, having been a member of a Junior Orange Lodge as a youngster. This was not an exceptional thing for a Protestant child to do in a rural area of Northern Ireland. There was no thought that belonging to the Order was in any way a political act. It was quite simply a part of life, made the easier because my father, uncles and grandfather on both sides of the border had been members before me.

Without wanting to lapse into the sentimental retrospection that mourns for the times when you could leave your backdoor unlocked and neighbour always helped neighbour, being a member of the Orange Order was quite an ordinary thing to do. Memories of these times are of the annual family outing to the Twelfth of July demonstration, meat teas in church halls, extra pocket money to spend, and all interspersed by mildly boring church services on the Sunday before the Twelfth.

Reminiscing about the Orange Order on the basis of this experience is generally a positive exercise. It is to picture ordinary, generally decent, people engaged in pleasant if sometimes banal activity. It is to have memories of what was simply a part of our background and culture in a way not designed to be set over against others.

Although membership of the Order lapsed from those childhood days little seemed to happen to interfere with the memory of what was experienced as a harmless part of culture. However,

a social night out in Belfast in the early 1980s brought an unexpected disturbance. On the way to meet some friends, we made
our way out from Belfast city centre, and along the route found
ourselves being asked to pull our car to the side due to an on-
coming parade.

There was nothing threatening or unpleasant about the
prospect of meeting an Orange Parade. I was merely coming
face to face with something that had been a normal part of my
own cultural roots. What followed was as unexpected as it was
shocking. Police landrovers were parked along the ends of side
streets that led on to the parade route, in an attempt to keep two
sides apart. As the Orange parade passed along the road it was
obvious all was not well. Insults were traded between people on
both sides, occasional bottles thrown and obscene gestures
made by people taking part in the parade.

As a witness who had no experience or knowledge of the
nuances of this particular situation, and who was not instinctively threatened by Orange culture, an unexpected reaction occurred. Instinct won over sensibility. In the emotional shock of
what I had just witnessed, I made my way behind the landrovers
to several groups of ordinary people who were standing nearby.
Attempting to contain my emotion I simply stated that I was a
Protested clergyman and that I was shocked and outraged by
what I had just witnessed. As a Protestant clergyman I offered
my apologies for what had just taken place. The incident passed,
but a new memory and experience had been added.

As someone who had grown up in a rural part of Northern
Ireland, experience of Twelfth of July demonstrations was limited
to those held in small towns and villages. On only one occasion
had our family made the long journey to Belfast for the Twelfth
of July demonstration. As a childhood memory it is one of a big
family day out. It was to be almost three decades later before I
witnessed another Twelfth demonstration in Belfast. This time I
went as one of the organisers of a Residential Conference. The
purpose of the Residential, organised by ECONI,[1] was to enable
a very varied group of people to have a meaningful engagement

with Orange culture.

The opportunity of being at the Belfast Twelfth of July demonstration left me with a number of uncomfortable impressions. I reflected as someone who had a disposition to enjoy the music and colourful spectacle of such an event. Watching as the demonstration passed it was impossible not to notice the unmistakeable paramilitary trappings and flavour of some of those who participated in the parade. Moving on to the Field itself gave the opportunity to browse amongst the various stalls that must have obviously been licensed in some way by the parade organisers. Not only did stalls provide the opportunity to buy a hamburger or something to quench the thirst, but also to buy items that celebrated paramilitary activity. At the bottom of the Field was the religious service followed by speeches, seemingly ignored by all but a tiny group of people. Experiencing this demonstration raised the question as to how it was that the parade was allowed to contain elements that had an overt paramilitary flavour, and that items celebrating paramilitary activity were being openly sold from stalls in the Field? This lent a dimension to the event that made it less than a benign family day out.

How might one collate or make sense of these different experiences of the Orange Order? In one way the personal participation gave a strong sense that the Order was a genuinely benign and legitimate expression of culture. What was personally observed on other occasions produced a strong sense of uneasiness, and serious questions about the compatibility of what was experienced with basic Christian principles. If there is this confusion in a Northern Protestant who is used to, and by background not threatened by, the Orange Order, then what may be the experiences of someone who is not from such a background?

CHAPTER ONE

Being of Sound Mind:
Asking the Right Questions

Many will question the need to discuss the relationship between the Church of Ireland and the Orange Order at all. Some will contend that there has been a relationship for such a long time, and one which is part and parcel of the fabric of many local communities, that there is nothing to discuss. Others take strong exception to the Order and will simply argue that there should be no visible relationship whatsoever. So why is the nature of the relationship between the two a matter worthy of discussion?

The context in which any church is called to live out an authentic Christian witness in Northern Ireland is one of a divided society. Conflict has been played out in many guises over the years. At times it has found its expression in overt acts of violence to both people and property. At other times the guise has changed, with deep community tensions and divisions finding their expression in other ways. The issue of parades has become an overtly potent issue in the community over recent years.

Parading is the public expression of Orangeism. The pretext may be the Twelfth of July, the Battle of the Somme anniversary, a District Parade or whatever. Orange parades may be to a church or be wholly unrelated. Not every Orange parade is an expression of conflict, as the statistics of the Parades Commission bear out. In terms of mere statistics, the instances where the Commission has had to impose restrictions is relatively small. A great number pass off unremarkably and undisputed. However, the issue of parades as a matter of contention has become a matter of increasing public attention in recent years.

There are varieties of parades and the Orange Order or the unionist communities are not exclusive practitioners. Not all parades within the Protestant or unionist community are to be associated with the Orange Order. There is the frequent phenomenon of Band Parades. Although often mistakenly associated with the Order, they are in fact something quite different. They are, as the very name suggests, parades that are organised by a local band with other bands being invited to participate. It is recognised that many of the bands that will participate in such an event will also be used to lead lodges at Orange demonstrations. The atmosphere at a Band Parade may range from an enjoyable musical spectacle to something much more intimidating, depending on the particular event.

Wherever conflict is played out in Northern Ireland, symbolism is serious business. We can note, without prejudice, that many Orange Order parades are to and from Church of Ireland churches. With the obvious exception of Drumcree, these occasions are generally unremarkable and peaceful. However, the fact that parades have become an issue of contention in recent years, for whatever reason, make the issue of the relationship between the Church of Ireland and the organisation that organises most parades to church services a reasonable matter for discussion. It does not presuppose a conclusion, but reflection on the issue is certainly warranted.

The recurring crisis at Drumcree has thrown the relationship between the Church of Ireland and the Orange Order into sharp focus. No longer a localised dispute, it is being played out before a worldwide audience. We are watching prime time television as the storms have gathered around the dispute on a seemingly annual basis. Whatever may be the underlying issues of that particular dispute, it is unmistakably linked with a Church of Ireland parish church, and hence with the church itself.

There are those who argue that any parade dispute is linked only to what happens after members of the Orange Order have left a church service. It is therefore argued that the Church of Ireland can have no responsibility for what takes place beyond its gates involving the actions of those, wearing full regalia, who have attended the service as a group.

Disassociation after the fact is hardly convincing! The Church of Ireland, and Drumcree parish, cannot claim the role of mere observers operating from a vantagepoint of glorious isolation. It has become the cause of debate and soul searching at all levels of the Church of Ireland. This debate has shown deep differences, ranging from the approach of such groups as Catalyst, who are highly critical of the Orange Order, to members of the church who are openly supportive of the Order at Drumcree. It has also opened up north-south tensions within the Church of Ireland. The fact that such a dispute exists at Drumcree, with all the attendant violent incidents that have occurred, make the matter of the relationship between the Orange Order and the Church of Ireland a matter of urgent discussion.

Drumcree most certainly provides a dramatic backdrop for discussing the relationship between the Church of Ireland and the Orange Order. It has inspired strong passions on all sides of the argument. Beyond Drumcree there is the reality that any such relationship is often worked out in mundane ways in parishes throughout Northern Ireland. This is expressed in the holding of Orange services, the fact that members of the Order are often active parishioners, and the display of flags and other emblems at particular times of the year. Away from the passions that surround Drumcree, there is the reality of many law abiding faithful parishioners who are members of the Orange Order for what they believe are honourable, or indeed ordinary motives.

Some clergy are active members of the Orange Order whilst others are not, but happily accede to requests for services or such like. Other clergy are reluctant or confused about acquiescence. There are others who will simply not entertain any service associated with the Orange Order at their church. As regards a small section of the Church of Ireland in Northern Ireland, it is not an issue that has to be faced. As has been noted, the experience of the Orange Order by different people in

Northern Ireland will vary from person to person. South of the border it is not a matter that greatly impinges on day to day parish life, though that is not to say that there are not strong feelings on the matter.

Christians are called to have a witness to all people.[2] Christians are also called to be good neighbours.[3] To assert these simple foundational truths is not immediately to predict conclusions to the matter under discussion. However, it does mean that the perceptions and experiences of those sections of the community that do not belong to the Church of Ireland, or indeed to the Protestant community, are relevant matters for consideration.

The issues highlighted in the relationship between the Church of Ireland and the Orange Order have significance and urgency in the light of Drumcree. Whatever the pressures of the moment the question remains: What is an appropriate relationship between the Church of Ireland and the Orange Order? The practical impact of the answers to this question is not to be underestimated. But to answer the question requires a move away from prejudice and the politics of the pressure of the moment. The matter must be assessed on the basis of sound criteria.

The Orange Order is an emotive issue in Northern Ireland. All too often people tend to react on an emotional level when discussing it. To reflect on the issue of an appropriate relationship between the Church of Ireland and the Orange Order is hardly less emotive or delicate. Any side of the conflict in our community is given to great, and perhaps excessive, sensitivity when they are analysed. One wonders what the outcome for any organisation including the Church of Ireland would be if it were to be subject to the same exhaustive and painstaking analysis. The same might be asked if it were a Catholic or nationalist organisation placed under the unrelenting gaze of the spotlight. To ask questions is all too quickly seen as attack. Nevertheless, the question still stands.

Reaction to this issue on a purely emotional level will simply not do. Great heat is not the equivalent of adding great light to a matter, and will tend to obscure more than illuminate. So the need for a move away from emotional reaction and mere rhetoric is definitely called for. Nor is it good enough to suggest that just because a relationship in some shape or form may have existed in the past that a continuation of the status quo, with no questions asked, is an adequate response to the question. However, if emotion and unthinking adherence to the status quo do little justice to the quest for answers, then what will?

The answer is simplicity itself. The Church of Ireland must respond as a Christian church to this matter. Most simply this means that, faced with a complex matter, it is wise that any response should have a solid theological foundation. If this is not done there is the temptation to respond to the heat of the moment or to the demands of others. If there is not the grounding of a reasonable theological framework, then it is more likely that the response may owe more to competing political considerations. With a sound theological foundation it is possible to formulate a policy that will produce a strategy, and ultimately good practice on the ground.

Getting right answers requires asking right questions. A first priority is to examine the substance of what the Church of Ireland and the Orange Order *are* as organisations. It is to distil the very essence of what both organisations are by nature, and to understand their *raison d'être*. Having done this, the next step will be to consider whether there are key biblical principles and foundational teachings from the New Testament words of Jesus that are directly relevant to an examination of the relationship between the two bodies. Great care must be taken in this matter. There is an easy temptation to use and abuse scripture in the cause of an argument, from whatever side. Having established the nature of both organisations, and isolated relevant biblical teaching, a further appropriate factor in determining a relationship is to reflect on the ethos of both organisations, and consider areas of compatibility or otherwise.

Yet there are other layers of considerations to be placed on the solid foundation of a theological reflection on the issue. It is surely relevant to the matter in question to have some reflection on community relations issues as they may affect any such relationship. Whilst clearly understanding that wider political considerations must not be the foundation for defining a relationship, it would nevertheless be irresponsible to overlook the influence that these might bring to bear. In all of this, there must be an appreciation of the implications on the ground for working out the practice of our theology. Standing at a safe distance can lend great enthusiasm to our calls for someone else to walk the way of the cross!

The Essence of Orangeism:
Why Does the Order Exist?

Getting an answer to this question will depend very much on who is asked! That being said, the institution is generally recognised to have four different strands to its *raison d'être*. At different times it may be characterised as having a political, religious, cultural or historical dimension. The Order should not be seen exclusively as one or other of these, but that it may be regarded as a mixture of all of them. The crucial debate centres on which of these aspects is mostly to the fore.

I. TELLING A HISTORY?

Understanding the essence of the Orange Order requires some attempt at historical context. It may come as a surprise to those outside the Orange Order, but 1690 and the Battle of the Boyne did not mark the birth date of the Orange Order. The actual birth came over one hundred years after this event, in 1795.

As is stated in the report of the Standing Committee of the 1999 General Synod:

> The Loyal Orange Institution may be said to derive from three sources – the Williamite Societies such as the Boyne Society; the Volunteers; and the Orange Boys formed at the Dyan in Tyrone by James Wilson.[4]

The Orange Order was founded in county Armagh at a time of agrarian land struggles. In eighteenth century Armagh the linen industry was beginning to upset longstanding structured inequalities between Catholics and Protestants. This led

Protestant weavers to attack Roman Catholics for breaking through traditional limits in the local economic field. The tensions of this situation led to rural vendettas and faction fights that were primarily of local and personal character rather than religious or political on a grand scale. The end of the eighteenth century saw land and the competing struggle for ownership of land in Ireland as an important issue. The population had increased significantly and this led to increased competition for land. Particularly in Armagh the population was evenly divided between Protestant and Catholic communities, both hungry for land. This situation gave rise to various skirmishes and occasional outrages perpetrated by factions or societies on both sides of the community. Distant history to us it may be, but to the communities of that time the conflict and possible outcome was of crucial importance.

A skirmish at the Diamond on 21 September 1995 in north county Armagh followed an attempt by the Defenders, a Catholic organisation, to hold an armed demonstration. The Defenders were dominating parts of the countryside at that time, with Protestant groups such as the Peep O' Days not proving a great match for them. If the Defenders had succeeded, Protestants at that time would have perceived it as a serious matter for them. The resulting armed skirmish led to a compact being made by a number of Protestants to form a defensive organisation. M. M. Ross comments on the mindset of the founders of this new institution:

> They realised that individual loyalty and zeal could never meet the imminent dangers of the country, and that it was only when people became part of an organisation that they became strong.[5]

A. T. Q. Stewart describes the birth of the Orange Order as
… The consequence of prolonged and severe sectarian conflict lasting for twenty years in a part of Armagh.[6]

It was called the Orange Society as a compliment to King William III. The challenge was to provide something simple enough for men to understand but strong enough to keep them together. In this manner the Orange Order was born. Whatever manifestations it may have since then, it originated as a defensive organisation to band together an insecure community in the midst of bitter struggle for land.

A strong religious or spiritual motive is not particularly apparent in the formation of the Orange Order and the initial setting up of Grand Lodge in 1798. However, what started as a peasant organisation began to be taken over by the leaders of Protestant society, namely gentry and the clergy. As documents were drawn up the aspect of religion was brought more to the fore. Perhaps there was the sense that a strong peasant organisation could be a dangerous thing and that religious influence might help to moderate it. Conceivably there was the feeling that a religious aspect could help to channel very obvious passion. It could also be argued that clergy felt that here was an organisation that had the potential for good or evil, so let it be for good. Whatever the conjecture, if the initial motive was defence in a struggle for land, the religious aspect only became more prominent in the early years of its existence. It would seem difficult to argue that religion was the core driving force behind the setting up of the organisation, but rather that the initial development of this dimension in its history was fortuitous.

II. EXPRESSING AN IDENTITY – ORANGEISM AND THE PROTESTANT PSYCHE
There is a strong celebratory element to the Orange Order. Celebration takes place as a way of remembering events in history seen as key in the development of their community. However, there is another aspect to collective acts of celebration. It is not so much that particular events are remembered for their historical significance, it is that they also provide profound metaphors for any community to describe life as they perceive it in the present.

A sense of identity is a knowledge of who one is, where one has come from, and how one is placed in the world. It is not only individuals who need a sense of identity. Communities have similar needs. Identity is something that is shaped not just by the present, but also by the past. The ability to know who one is and where one is going will be greatly aided by some sense of the road that has already been travelled. This is why history is such a vital part of the life of any community. If only the retelling of history was as simple as isolating and collating bare facts! Yet, especially in any situation of conflict, the way in which 'facts' are perceived and the values that are bestowed on them can make historical analysis very much a subjective exercise. This is illustrated in any consideration of the conflict in Northern Ireland.

When communities in Northern Ireland recount their past it is often not so much a case of the objective retelling of historical 'truths', as interpreting events in a way that reinforces the story of that particular community. History provides for each community not just a record of events but a series of metaphors to describe the past, present and future. History has supplied dominant themes in the psychology of all communities in Northern Ireland and has provided central paradigms that shape reaction and perception to the present day.

A. T. Q. Stewart emphasises that the appeal to history is not an entirely objective exercise as he notes:

> … the Irish are not only capable of forgetting the past, but quite deliberately expunging from their minds whole areas of it. Like other nations they have woven for themselves a garment of myth and legend which they call Irish history. Having designed it themselves, they have taken great care to make it as comfortable as possible.[7]

Stewart describes the past as 'a convenient quarry which provides ammunition to use against enemies in the present'.[8] History becomes myth when it ceases to be concerned solely with objective study of the past and becomes, even subconsciously, a telling of a story to make sense of the life of a community. It is all too easy for any community to impute sacredness to historical events where the complexities of the time are forgotten and a metaphor is formed for the sake of the present.

In Protestant Orange culture the story of a faithful remnant under siege, and the richness of sacrifice, is retold year by year in the July parades. The symbolism of the Orange banners and the telling of the stories of the past bring the observer back to the days of Elijah, Gideon's faithful men, heathens and foreigners against the chosen few, the Siege of Derry, and to the Somme. Familiar biblical texts are used to provide a focus for symbolic ritual activity. They are often used on such occasion to show relevance to the contemporary social, religious, and political issues in Northern Ireland. They become metaphors for the way in which Orangeism sees the situation of the Protestant community in the present. The themes are a constant reminder of conflict, betrayal and siege. As one views the passing Orange banners one remembers that the stories of yesterday are only different from the interpretations of today in the detail.

It is not unnatural that history, metaphor and myth are part of the story of any community. However, the ideas of the past that are thus contained play a crucial part in contemporary politics and life in Northern Ireland. The problem arises when these are uncritically accepted. Sadly Orangeism is not unique in Northern Ireland in that its view of history is at times selective, incomplete and inaccurate. History thus turns to myth and ends up obscuring reality.

The appeal to history that helps shape the Orange psyche is no less a result of a selective view of the past than in any other community. The way in which history can give way to something that approaches myth can be seen in the perceptions of some of the most definitive dates in Irish history.

The Battle of the Boyne is the inspiration for the Twelfth of July Orange celebrations that take place across Northern Ireland each year. This Battle of the Boyne, and the military campaign that accompanied it, has passed into folklore as one of the decisive battles in the struggle between William of Orange and King James II. The events of these years resonate deeply in the hearts and minds of many within the unionist community, yet the intricacies of the events surrounding the struggles of the time are not often paid heed to. The events are seen as being a struggle between the Catholic forces of King James and the Protestant forces of William of Orange. Seen in this way it seems like a very simple fight, not only between Protestantism and Catholicism, but implicitly between good and evil. Yet the battles being fought in Ireland at this time were really part of a much greater and more complicated power play. It was not just a struggle for the English throne but also part of ongoing dispute, albeit by proxy, between major European powers. The fact that the pope felt it appropriate to celebrate a Mass in thanksgiving for the victory of William of Orange makes it rather less clear-cut as a simple battle between Protestantism and Catholicism. In fact some of William's finest troops were Catholic.

Trying to deal with the present can be a difficult task when the burden of history is ever present. Allowing the metaphors of the past to shape the present creates a sense of fatalism and confrontation, rather than compromise and peaceful coexistence. Alvin Jackson makes a somewhat gloomy assessment as he suggests:

> A particular sense of history and a particular cast of mind permit the present to be fulfilled by the events of a long dead struggle.[9]

Frank Wright uses some historical observation to isolate a recurring theme:

> Ulster Unionists opposing the Home Rule Bills of 1886, 1893 and 1912 used to say that their society had been permanently under siege since its plantation or colonial origins in the seventeenth century. This continual sense of siege has been recognised by historians as the central reality of Northern Protestant society.[10]

Siege has been one of the most obvious paradigms to describe this community from the days of the plantation until the present. A community is under siege when it is surrounded by what it perceives to be a hostile enemy. Accompanying this state of affairs will be a sense of being alone or abandoned. It is a case of the embattled community against the enemy. Victory comes simply by being able to hold out. An essential part of being able to hold out is to keep the embattled community united and to raise the ramparts as a means of protection. Survival in and of itself is victory.

The telling of the story is a strong dimension of Orangeism. So much of the activity and public demonstration involves the telling and retelling of a history that is not only for the sake of remembrance but is meant to have strong resonance for present day situations. The presence of celebration within the psyche of Orange culture and practice is as much as anything about celebrating survival.

Deep within the psyche of Orangeism is the memory of battles still capable of being remembered by the few survivors. These are the battles of the First World War. The Somme still manages to resonate deeply within the psyche of the Ulster Orangeman, with all the images of sacrifice and suffering. To observe some of the banners at a Twelfth demonstration, or even to note the resemblance of some band uniforms with First World War army uniforms, is to realise the continuing power and profound affect of such memory.

The historical dimension of Orangism functions in the same way as the retelling of past stories for so many communities of people. The jogging of historical memory by constant retelling of the story helps generate a sense of meaning for a community. Recounting the stories of struggles by fathers and forefathers, whether at the Boyne or the Somme, is used as inspiration for the present. The danger with an uncritical retelling of the past is that it turns into an unconscious reliving of the same in the present. Ruth Dudley Edwards describes such danger thus:

> To the opposing tribes of Ireland, Irish history is but a tool in the fashioning of identity and a weapon in the long war.[11]

Walker makes similar observation:

> Historical knowledge can help illuminate our situation today, but it is essential that we do not allow a selective and inaccurate understanding of the past to set the agenda and

compound our problems.[12]

The constant public retelling of a historically flawed version of history allows one community to celebrate its 'innocence' in the face of another. This theme is not only good for the past, but interprets the present. A celebrating of 'innocence' as implied in an Orange retelling of history is not compatible with an organisation publicly committed to the Christian faith, the founder of which declares that only a person without sin is qualified to cast the first stone.

III. POLITICS AND THE ORDER

In its early years the Orange Order remained essentially a minority movement amongst Protestants. The rural roots of the organisation were still to be seen as the economic competition from the Catholic population and relaxation of the Penal Code seemed at times to threaten the privileges of Protestant rural tenantry. In this sense it could be argued that the Order contributed to a sense of cohesion and identity for this grouping. However, there was little interest from the commercial or professional Protestant classes. At other times it seemed that apathy was the most potent danger that the Order faced in terms of its existence. This, however, was to change with the political atmosphere in Ireland at the end of the nineteenth century. There was one issue that would dominate the political landscape in Ireland at that time and that was Home Rule.

The history of Orangeism is that it rises in prominence when the Protestant or pro-union population in Ireland perceives itself to be under threat. Home Rule was the very essence of such threat. Between 1874 and 1883 the Land League and Home Rule parties in Ireland were beginning to have noticeable impact and success. It was this success and a consequent rising insecurity in the Protestant population that encouraged a turning to Orangeism as a defensive organisation.

Up until this time there had been mixed fortunes for the Orange Order. There had been little apparent social prestige for it and the bulk of membership was made up of small farmers and agricultural labourers. However, the Home Rule crisis saw moves by middle class Protestants to become part of the Orange Institution. It was a crisis that saw the Order transformed from a somewhat plebeian fraternal organisation into a potent political force, and from a minority movement amongst Protestants into something more mainstream.

The birth of unionism took place in the midst of struggle over one issue. The redrawing of the political landscape in Ireland during the last decades of the nineteenth century came down to the core issue of whether Ireland should continue in its constitutional position with Great Britain. It was the reorganising of the Catholic population in Ireland, initially energised by the land issue, that was the catalyst for the formation of the Unionist Party to resist the pressure for Home Rule. The years from 1870 onwards were to see the emergence of a specifically unionist party within Ireland. The events surrounding the issue of Home Rule, the attempts of Gladstone to bring the issue through parliament, and the numerous elections of these years brought about a transformation of party politics in Ireland.

The issue of Home Rule was to crystallise the differences within Ireland. As this issue gathered momentum constitutional politics became party politics. Party politics in turn became confessional politics. The land question was one that had been a driving force in the formation of nationalist politics. This converged with the influence of Gladstone. He was a politician who became determined to solve the Irish Question. It became apparent to him that the way of doing this was to grant Home Rule.

In 1879 the Irish National Land League was founded. It embodied some of the latent desires of the Catholic population, with the hope of dismantling the power of the landlords. The slogan 'Land for the people' took on a political meaning and Home Rule took on a momentum. Increasingly the Land movement was identified with Home Rule. This aspiration was something that was largely Catholic.

The General Election of 1874 saw the election of sixty Home

Rule MPs. In 1885 the number was eighty-six. This period saw a new cohesion coming into nationalist politics. As Irish nationalism began to develop it seemed to embody the hopes of Irish Catholics for the future as well as supplying motifs for the past. The effect of the development of the new forms which Catholic nationalism was taking, combined with the efforts of Gladstone, resulted in the development of unionism. It was the threat of an increasingly coherent nationalism and the unpredictability of parliamentary support in Westminster that gave rise to conviction of the need for a coherent unionist political movement. It was in these years, including the Ulster Unionist Convention of 1892, that unionism began to be a coherent political force in its own right.

The period between 1886 and 1911 was one of rising political tension for the pro-union community. In the context of the Home Rule crisis, that spanned from 1886 to the early 1920s, the Orange Order adopted, or had thrust upon it, the mantle of a strong backbone of resistance. The most public form of this opposition to Home Rule came in the form of the decision in 1885 by Grand Lodge that a separate parliamentary party needed to be formed to protect the union. It was thus out of the intimate substance of the Orange Order that the Unionist Party came into being. Links between the Ulster Unionist Party and the Orange Order that exist to this day have their roots in the birth of the Unionist Party.

Between 1886 and 1922 the Orange Order provided a strong backbone for the anti Home Rule movement in Ireland. In 1795 it had been the concerns of the labouring and poorer artisan Protestant classes that provided the seedbed for the birth of the Orange Order. With the threat of Home Rule at the end of the nineteenth century gentry, clergy, business interests and farmers came on board with their religious and economic objections to Home Rule. A. T. Q. Stewart remarks:

> The Orange Order provided a convenient framework, not only for political organisation, but if need be for a private army.[13]

In a real sense Orangeism fathered the Unionist Party. Not only was Orangeism at the core of setting up a unionist party in 1885 when it was decided to form a separate parliamentary party, it also helped to provide something more intangible yet profound. Jarman summarises the essence as he comments:

> At a time when Unionism was emerging as a distinct political response to nationalism, it needed to define itself clearly, to create and refine its myths and symbols, and state what made 'Ulster' distinct from Ireland.[14]

Many of the links between the Ulster Unionist Party and the Order that exist today date from the circumstances of the late nineteenth century. This includes the fact that the Order has the right to nominate one hundred and twenty delegates to the Ulster Unionist Council, the ruling body of the party. This intimacy, forged in the birth of unionism, and the fact that the Order was an exclusively Protestant organisation, has greatly fuelled the perception that Protestantism is synonymous with unionism, and that unionism is exclusively Protestant.

Whether it was in the setting up of an organisation for mutual defence in the midst of agrarian land disputes, as a key influence in the birth of the Unionist Party, or as a power that comes to the fore at times of perceived threat for the unionist population, the political dimension is there to see.

One need not depend on hearsay or the vagaries of personal opinion when considering the various aspects of the Orange Order. The specifics of the political dimensions of the Order are detailed in the *Basis of the Institution*. This states that the Order is an institution committed to 'support and defend the rightful sovereign'. The publication makes clear that such defence of the rightful sovereign means the support and defence of the succession to the throne in the House of Windsor.

Defence of civil and religious liberty is a recurrent theme in Orangeism. The defence of civil liberty moves beyond defence of the rightful sovereign, to the fact that the organisation bands members together for the defence of their own persons and properties. Having detailed commitment to the rightful sovereign and to the defence of its own membership, it then declares that part of the basis for the existence of the Institution is for the maintenance of the public peace.

There is tremendous emphasis on the position of Royalty, with all its symbols. The Order believes freedoms are only absolutely guaranteed by keeping a Protestant crown in Great Britain, which must therefore be defended. These freedoms are both civil and religious with the strong contention that this political state of affairs is necessary particularly for the preservation of religious freedoms. Dewar expresses some of the thinking behind the desire for this particular political context:

> … the Orange Institution is a voluntary association of English speaking Protestants …. In defence of civil and religious liberty … (with the object in 1795) … to aid and assist all loyal subjects of every religious persuasion, by protecting them from violence and oppression.[15]

He continues:

> …the true Orangeman of today, deeply loyal to the British crown and a faithful Protestant, is bound to support our constitutional system which maintains the Protestant religion and preserves the union between Great Britain and Northern Ireland. The border is as secure a bulwark to his religious faith and his political freedom.[16]

History makes it impossible to dispute that the Orange Order has a profound political dimension. That is to say political, not in a broad non-partisan sense, but as specifically unionist. Membership of the Orange Order includes a wide breadth of party allegiance that will be definitely unionist in sentiment. This is a perception both within and without the Institution. When asked if the Order was pro-unionist in character, one member voiced the view that there was 'no two ways about it'.[17] *Irish Times* journalist Patsy McGarry voiced the same opinion when he observed that the Order was 'unmistakably a unionist organisation'.[18]

IV. DEFENDING RELIGION

The Education Committee of the Grand Orange Lodge of Ireland states:

> The Orange Order is fundamentally a Christian organisation, as the *Basis of the Institution* states: 'The Institution is composed of Protestants, united and resolved to the utmost of their power to support and defend ... the Protestant Religion.'[19]

The religious dimension of the Order stands very much in the Reformed Protestant tradition. The Education Committee looks to the *Qualifications of an Orangeman* to flesh out what this may mean in practice for its membership. Four foundational principles are elucidated. The first principle is that of love for God, in the form of 'a sincere love and veneration for the heavenly Father'. This is followed by the need for faith in Christ in the sense of 'steadfast faith in Jesus Christ, the Saviour of mankind'.

Having laid this foundation of love for God and faith in Christ, it continues with assertion of the authority of scripture. The committee suggests that this be not merely in the sense of a general belief in the authority of the Bible. Its brief commentary rather states that such belief should be expressed in a member honouring and diligently studying scripture to 'make them the rule of his faith and practice'. It is clear that the standard by which any member should live his or her life is by that of the Bible.

The final principle alluded to is that of respect for Sunday. The *Qualifications* as quoted point out that members should 're-member to keep holy the Sabbath day, and attend the public worship of God'. Not only is it important that members respect Sunday as being a special day, there is also the clear injunction to attend a service of worship. The necessity of expressing personal faith by associating with other Christians in the context of regular public worship is clearly expressed.

The *Basis of the Institution*, as quoted by the Education Committee, declares of the Order:

> It is exclusively an Association of those who are attached to the religion of the Reformation, and will not admit into its brotherhood persons whom an intolerant spirit leads to persecute, injure, or upbraid any man on account of his religious opinions.[20]

In this sense it is clear that the doctrinal basis for the Orange Order is quite orthodox Reformation teaching. It is explicitly stated that not only is a core principle of the Orange Order that of upholding such teaching, but that this will not involve any intolerant attitude expressed against those of different opinion. Doctrinal orthodoxy is not all that is important, but also the attitude to others regardless of whether they are in agreement or not.

In practice the Orange Order functions as something of a para-church organisation. At lodge meetings prayers will be said and readings from the Bible. Each lodge has a chaplain, with Grand Chaplains for the lodge on a national level. Protestant clergy occupy many of these positions. Most of these lodges will have annual parades to church services on the Sunday before the Twelfth of July. These services will either be specially organised outside of normal service times, or members will parade to a normal service and attend as a lodge. At most Orange services to a church the Order will parade in full regalia and accompanied by flags and standards, including the Union Jack. It is not unusual to conclude these events by the singing of the National Anthem. At the Twelfth of July demonstrations a religious service will form a key, if on occasion sparsely attended, part of events at the Field. These services will consist of hymns, Bible readings, prayers and exposition from the Bible.

Depending on the character of individual lodges, some may organise Bible classes for members or run evangelistic events such as missions. Although this *may* be the case, it is not necessarily universal practice. Some lodges are quite active in this regard and at least one interviewee stated that he had come to personal Christian faith through the evangelistic endeavours of a lodge.[21]

The use of the Bible is prominent in the Orange Order. As has been stated, the *Qualifications of an Orangeman* call for acceptance of the authority of the Bible and use of it as a rule for faith and practice. Apart from the use of the Bible in lodge meetings and public services, it is also obvious at parades. Most lodges will have their own banners to accompany them at parades. Occasionally these will depict a local church building, portraits of King William III or a local dignitary. Yet more often than not the pictures will depict recurrent biblical themes or characters. Common amongst these are motifs that remind the observer of the theme of God's people as the chosen few protected from the enemy.

The Institution is sometimes the place where members find their greatest source of Christian fellowship. Church is meant to function as a place not only of nurture and outreach, but of Christian companionship. Unfortunately, the reality often provides little of real sustenance or warmth for members. This can be even more the case for male members of churches. Thus it can be that a lodge meeting provides a level of companionship and warmth that the local church fails to.

The Order characterises itself as an Institution committed to promoting the Protestant Reformed faith. It sees itself as uniting Protestants

> ... of all the Reformed denominations in opposition to biblical error and the encouragement of scriptural truth.[22]

Part of this involves it in specific opposition to Roman Catholicism. The theological reasons for this are the belief that Roman Catholic teaching contains much that is believed to be in error as regards biblical faith. Beliefs such as transubstantiation, Marianism, papal infallibility, as well as the Mass would fall into this category. It is the belief in Orangeism that such teachings are so contrary to Reformation teaching that they must be actively opposed. In that sense, the opposition to doctrinal error is not merely general in character but quite specific to the teachings of the Roman Catholic Church.

Its opposition to specifically Roman Catholic teaching leads the Order to being quite opposed to ecumenism with regard to the Roman Catholic Church. There is a sense that Protestantism is under threat and retreat. Over against this there is often the perception that the Roman Catholic Church is somehow unchanging and monolithic. This context is often accompanied by the suspicion that some Protestant clergy are diluting Protestantism by being involved in ecumenical dialogue or contact. The underlying thought is that true Protestantism can have no compromise with error. A more extreme version of this is that the Roman Catholic Church is an evil organisation that has to be defended against.

What marks Orangeism as particularly noteworthy is the link which it brings between defence of Reformed faith and the need for Northern Ireland to maintain union with Great Britain. In this sense it combines a theological or doctrinal understanding of faith with a particular political viewpoint. A key value for Orangeism is the maintenance of the relationship with Great Britain, as opposed to being part of an independent united Ireland. There is nothing remarkable in that as a political aspiration, except that it is linked to the defence of the gospel or Reformed faith.

The scripture is used not just to bring coherence to doctrinal orthodoxy. It can be used to make sense of present circumstances. Biblical concepts and imagery are important in framing the way of perceiving the world for the Orange Order. But are the images and concepts that are used to describe God's people in the scripture to be transferable so as to describe a particular people living in Northern Ireland at the end of the twentieth century and the beginning of the twenty first?

The Old Testament provides much symbolism and motif for Orangeism. If one examines such themes that this symbolism suggests one can see echoes in political expression. John Dickinson remarks:

Political symbolism, the endless marking of territory and the importance of holy places are just some aspects of Ulster Protestant life which are reminiscent of the Old Testament.[23]

One of the results of using such paradigms to describe more contemporary situations is that it can breed a sense of superiority. This is all the more so when attitudes that affect a sense of religious certainty with regard to truth begin to resonate with political matters.

The Order seamlessly weaves its political and religious dimensions. It argues that if the constitutional position of Northern Ireland within the United Kingdom were lost then civil and religious liberty would be endangered. It is reasoned that not only does the British crown provide a conducive atmosphere for the spreading of the gospel, but also an Irish Republic heavily influenced by Roman Catholicism would be more inhospitable for the practice of Reformed faith. Less flattering is to note that to be British is not normally a religious argument *per se*. It poses the question as to whether the Orange Order makes it so. It would seem to be the case that for some:

> ... geographical space and religious identity remain firmly intertwined; for them there is an intimate connection between territory and theology such that the preservation of the theology requires the maintenance of the geography.[24]

Were one to observe and analyse any Christian denomination it would not be possible to find a complete uniformity of character or level of Christian commitment. The Orange Order is no different in this respect. Analysing the membership will not reveal a totally homogeneous group of people. There are various levels of commitment that may be characterised in its membership. There are committed evangelical Christians who see the Order as a bastion of truth and an authentic presentation of the gospel. It is seen by these as a real opportunity to evangelise men in particular. After all, apart from Orange services it may be rare that a preacher would have a building full of men to evangelise at one time. For some even the right to parade has evangelistic significance, in that they feel that where there is freedom to march there is freedom to preach the gospel. The integrity of such an argument is surely best authenticated by inquiry to potential recipients of such evangelism.

For a great bulk of members, the religious dimension is present but less urgent. It is not that defence of the Reformed faith is disputed but rather that the reasons for their membership may be a lot more banal. Some members will be loyal members of their local church, with others perhaps claiming formal membership but rarely attending.

V. EXPRESSING CULTURE

One should not imagine that high in the consciousness of any member of the Orange Order is the fact that their organisation has religious, political and historical dimensions. As is the case with membership of so many organisations, including church, the reasons for association are often quite unremarkable. For many, membership of the Order is simply an ordinary part of their social and cultural life. It may not be so much an expression of Christian faith but rather a carrying on of family tradition. In this regard it owes more to being a part of the complex of things that help to make up the identity of any individual.

The type and expression of Orangeism as part of social life may vary between urban and rural lodges. For many men it is simply an opportunity to meet together with friends to talk about the ordinary things that any group of like-minded people might talk about. It may be less about great matters of Reformed faith, politics or conspiracy and more to do with cattle prices and ordinary conversation. It is a sad fact that church life for many Protestant men in particular often provides little such opportunity for enjoyable social interaction with one's peers. If the pub is not an alternative means of social life, then the lodge may be the thing to fill the gap. As one member of the Order described it:

> It is an opportunity for men to meet and discuss mutual interests.[25]

Much of the annual activity of lodges is taken up with regular lodge meetings, an annual church service and the occasional opportunity to dedicate banners and collarettes. For much of the membership this is pleasant and ordinary activity. Members argue that this activity is no less valid or different in principle than the holding of events such as Fleadhs or a Feis by members of other communities.

One must not be unaware of the dangers of sentimental retrospection in all of this. It is not to say that the other dimensions of the Orange Order do not exist or that any manifestation is never less than whiter than white. Perhaps it is rather to redress a balance that has been lost in much of the current observation and debate of the Institution. It is to make a simple point that, for many members, the Orange Order is an unremarkable part of their social life rather than a conscious means of expressing religious, political or historical points. It may be less a case of wanting to unite the faithful remnant than a simple exercise in male bonding.

Parades
The most public expression of Orangeism is parading. When asked to define what Orange culture is one may well be directed to parades, with all the attendant displays of banners, regalia, pageantry and musical prowess of the bands. For lodges and membership it is certainly the highpoint of annual activity. In terms of the social and cultural dimensions of Orangeism, this is certainly so. However, parading has also provided occasion for very public points of contention, most vividly expressed at Drumcree.

Public parades as culture are not the exclusive domain of the Orange Order. One may observe the parade of a Protestant uniformed organisation such as the Girls or Boys Brigade to see that marching and flags are part and parcel of what takes place. Neither is parading unique to the Protestant community. If parading is not necessarily a unique activity, let us consider the reasons for its practice. Jarman suggests that parading is a 'popular expression of cultural identity and difference'.[26] But apart from civil and religious liberty, what else is being celebrated?

We begin with consideration of what Orangeism itself believes is being legitimately expressed in parading.

A considered rationale for Orange parades is that they are celebrations. In general they are celebrations of Williamite victories that took place in the Ireland of the late seventeenth century. The Order will have various reasons as to why these victories should be celebrated. In particular the rationale of the Orange Order for such celebration is that Williamite victories guaranteed civil and religious liberty that remains until this day.

As one might expect, parading will encompass all of the various dimensions inherent in the Orange Order. They are expressions of identity and allegiance. One may list among the themes in Orange parades the celebration of political and cultural links with mainland Great Britain. To the Order a parade is a display of pageantry, but also an expression of a sense of tradition and a testimony and statement of beliefs.

Orangeism will feel that parades are expressions of legitimate pride in possession of their lands and liberties. The freedom to march the Queen's highway is to many members of the Order a symbol of the fact that in that place the writ of the crown is present.

In another regard they are celebrations of Protestant culture and survival in Ireland. It is not simply about the past, but also a statement about the determination to survive in the present. In specific local situations parading may be about showing local solidarity and strength and reminding the population on all sides about the right of free assembly and passage for Protestants in general and Orangemen in particular.

There are alternative ways of interpreting parading within the psyche of Orangeism. One may take the view that such events are a testimony to and united expression of the religion and political aspirations of a section of Protestant people. There are those marching who would not disagree with Ruth Dudley-Edwards in her assertion:

> For inarticulate and threatened people walking the territory is their way of expressing the link with the past.[27]

To many members of the Order and their families, parades are seen as a valid reason for a good day out. It is the stuff of meat teas, smart turnout and meeting friends. In all of the reflection on parading it is easy to be blind to this dimension, or to be fashionably cynical about its existence. To lose sight of this dimension of ordinary people engaged in ordinary, but to them pleasurable, activity is to fail to appreciate all the facets of parading.

The great majority of parades considered by the Parades Commission do not have strictures placed on them. Hundreds take place each year without public expressions of disapproval or disorder. However, the good old days when every parade always passed off without problem, benignly watched by Catholic neighbours, may have as much to do with folk memory as reality.

Whatever history may tell us it seems fair to say that, particularly since the 1960s, there has been an increased dimension of territoriality in this area of life in Northern Ireland. There are certainly alternative perceptions on the subject of parading in the community. Having noted those of the Orange Order, it seems fair to do the same for those who of an alternative disposition.

We have become tragically used to the spectacle of Drumcree each year, along with other scenes of dispute. Yet disorder and parading are not necessarily new phenomena. Instances in the nineteenth century in Belfast reveal times of disorder and riot connected with parading.

At its very heart there is a fear amongst some of the Catholic and nationalist community that parading has a less benign focus than that already noted. Parading or 'walking' was a phenomenon in the Protestant community prior to the birth of the Orange Order. In these instances, and in what followed with Orangeism, parades were most definitely not always conducted for recreational purposes. They were also in some way a ritual declaration of power or dominance, the ritual being expressed in the territory covered by the route.

The fear is that in essence parading has more to do with expressions of Protestant or Orange power and ownership. There is a nagging sense in some that what may be at the core of procession is an assertion of old rights and 'keeping the papists in their place'. There are those who may not have such a nuanced view but who nevertheless observe some of the manifestations of swagger displayed on occasion at Orange parades and feel not only distaste but intimidation. Observation of a distinct paramilitary flavour, such as observed by the author at the Belfast Twelfth demonstration,[28] vividly undermines an exclusively benign interpretation of all Orange parading.

SO WHAT IS THE ORANGE ORDER?

What is clear is that the Order is an organisation without one sole and exclusive dimension. As an Institution it brings together a number of shared values. These include belief in God, a commitment to Reformed Christian faith, civil and religious liberty, and a specific commitment and loyalty to the British State. None of these values are remarkable in their own right All are individually valid. What is more startling is the way in which these values have been enmeshed together to make something of a whole. In particular it is the linking between a commitment to Reformed faith and a specific political outlook, with the implication that the one is dependent on the other. A particular political loyalty becomes an article of religious faith! The constant retelling of the stories of 1688 to 1690 that are communicated with a collective sense of persecution, suffering, solidarity, divine providence, and eventual deliverance, have created an organisation that seeks to defend a status quo not only within the religious but also the civil arena.

Fraternity, or brotherhood, is a core theme within Orangeism. Fraternity is something that requires a set of common values that will unite an otherwise disparate group of people into a brotherhood. The key question is to identify what these common values are in essence. David Chillingworth, in reflecting on the essence of the Orange Order, described it as:

binding together of political, religious and cultural attitudes of settlers.[29]

It is unmistakable that commitment to Reformed faith is one
of the key elements within Orangeism. However, it is not the
only one. Along with it is a profound political dimension.
McDonald describes it as 'The most vivid expression of unionist
and British identity'.[30] This brings us to the key issue in describing the essence of the Orange Order, the combining of land and
theology. The Institution is a para-church organisation that
states that it exists for the good of the gospel. Yet it has a profound political dimension in its roots, history, core beliefs and
present practice. This poses the question as to whether it has to
do with something altogether more earthy, the desire to defend
land and identity.

Dean Griffin describes the Order as:

a pseudo religious political Order in defence of the
Protestant and Reformed faith, but with a belief that it cannot
survive without the prop of the union. It wraps the Bible in
the Union Flag.[31]

Among Protestants as a group there has been a fear going
back through many hundreds of years. This has essentially been
a fear for their own survival. Is it the fear for survival as an ethnic
group, or a passion for the gospel in Ireland, that is at the heart
of Orangeism? Is religion fortuitous or at the core of what it is?

What one seems to have is a religious element that is locked into
a political movement. It is as John Dickinson describes it, 'a
Christianised hybrid religious practice'.[32] In this regard the religious aspect gives a certain credence and authority to political and
social aspects. By no stretch of the imagination can it be claimed
that it is primarily a religious organisation with political ramific-
ations. The political dimension is profoundly at the core of what it is.

Understanding the true nature of the Orange Order requires
an understanding of the Protestant psyche. Protestantism is by
no means monolithic as an entity in Northern Ireland, and is actually quite fragmented. It is unfortunate that whilst liberalism in
many of its guises has not always tried to understand Protest-

antism, the same has often done itself no favours in presenting a cogent apologia.

There is an obsession with identity in Northern Ireland. No grouping including Christian denominations is immune to such fascination. Religion as well as politics has been embraced as one of the crucial identifiers for communities. Ulster Protestants as an ethnic group are defined as much as anything by their religion, regardless of the practice of it. As McGarry expresses it, 'Religion is the key ethnic marker'.[33]

Issues of land and identity are too familiar themes for all parts of the community in Northern Ireland. It is the picture of one group of people possessing land and wanting to hold on to it in the face of threat from another. Protestant insecurity is essentially that they will be overrun by the Catholic Irish and at the same time be abandoned by the British. In this desire to defend and maintain there is a lurking fear of what the pain of loss might actually feel like. It is ironic that one community does not realise that the sense of vulnerability it feels may be mirrored more than it realises in the other.

In the midst of the atmosphere of struggle there is a mixture of endurance, intransigence, a strong sense of principle, but also a profound insecurity within the Protestant psyche. Liam Clarke describes Protestants as being 'essentially pessimistic'. Dunn and Morgan elaborate on such an observation by noting that within Northern Protestants there is:

> a perception that within Northern Ireland the social and constitutional bulwarks and defences for Protestants are being steadily and persistently eroded.[34]

It is to such themes that the various dimensions of Orangeism give both expression and sustenance.

CHAPTER THREE

The Essence of the Church of Ireland?

Sometimes it helps to state the obvious. The very essence of the Church of Ireland is that it is a Christian church. Before it is anything else, or claims any other identity, its nature, reason for existence, and aims are inherently bound up in the character of Jesus Christ. It is as part of the worldwide body of Christ that it gains its most essential reason for existence.

The incarnation is expressed with a great economy of words in Matthew 1:23. The gospel writer describes the name by which the soon to be born Messiah would be known. He was to be called Immanuel, which means 'God with us'. As the man Jesus walked the earth in Palestine thus the incarnation was happening. God had come in amongst human beings in the form of his Son. How was it possible to actually see God in the middle of human existence? The answer was, and is, to look at the person of Jesus!

Following the death, resurrection, and the ascension of Jesus into heaven he was no longer going to be present on the earth in the form of that one human physical body. Christian theology teaches us that he is nevertheless present on the earth in a body. The difference is that the body he now manifests himself in on earth is not one physical body but the whole body of Christian believers together, collectively known as the church or the body of Christ. It is true that this manifestation has imperfections as Christ is using a collection of imperfect human beings as his body to live in. Nevertheless the simple point is that the nature and character of the Christian church is intended to be intimately related to the person and character of Jesus Christ. The Church of Ireland is to be no exception.

To state that the Church of Ireland at its most profound level is a Christian church is to assert that it is first and foremost meant to be a divine institution. If the Church of Ireland is a Christian church this means that Jesus Christ is the one who is head of that organisation. Allegiance is to be primarily to him before anyone or anything else. This allegiance will be expressed in its character, priorities and day to day activity. The 1999 General Synod was in agreement with this principle:

> The priority in any situation is to seek the mind and will of God. Which course of action brings honour to his name? Which decisions will facilitate his will being done on earth as it is in heaven? How is the Lordship of Christ to be expressed?[35]

It is recognised that the Christian church is divided into many denominations, each with different emphases either in doctrine or practice. Is it possible to isolate a number of key scriptural principles that must define the nature and life of any Christian church? The danger in seeking to isolate key biblical principles for such a purpose is that each denomination will have texts that are core to their understanding of church. It would therefore be impossible to give an exhaustive and incontrovertible list of key characteristics. What one may omit is perhaps of crucial importance for another.

Being mindful of the risks of such an enterprise, let us nevertheless suggest a number of seminal principles for the life and witness of any Christian church. To note these is not to say that such a list is exhaustive, yet it is to suggest that they are foundational in any understanding of church.

1. Identity
Controversy over doctrine and practice is not unique to the contemporary church. It is something that has existed from the very beginnings of the church in the New Testament. Although there was undoubtedly a power in the witness of the early Christians one could make the mistake of thinking that the times of the

New Testament were in some way idyllic and without controversy. Such was not the case.

Christ was a practising Jew. The first Christians were Jewish
by background. In the world of that time Jews would have seen
the world as being divided between two categories of people,
Jew and non-Jew. In the initial period of the Christian church
Jewish believers practised their Jewish religion by attending
synagogue and the Temple. There was no complication between
the two as long as one of two things continued to happen: that
these new believers continued to be accepted by the rest of the
Jewish community or that all new believers were exclusively
Jewish by background.

The most obvious initial activity of the early church was mission. It was inevitable that gentiles, or non-Jews, would be evan-
gelised and that some would declare faith in Christ. As this
began to happen controversy arose amongst some Christians. If
a gentile became a Christian would they also have to become a
Jew? Would this be necessary if Jewish Christians were to enjoy
full fellowship with them? After all, gentiles did not practise
Jewish rites and practices. Some Christians wondered if it made
them unclean if they were to have fellowship with, or even eat
with believers who were gentiles by background. Put another
way: was the world still to be divided into two categories, Jew
and gentile? It was into this controversy that the Letter to the
Galatians was written.

Paul expresses the answer to this controversial question in
his Letter to the Church at Galatia.

> You are all sons of God through faith in Christ Jesus, for all of
> you who were baptised into Christ have clothed yourselves
> with Christ. There is neither Jew not Greek, slave nor free,
> male nor female, for you are all one in Christ Jesus.[36]

Paul's teaching is self-explanatory. If a person put their faith
in Christ then they became, in a generic sense, sons of God. The
use of the phrase 'baptised into Christ' describes an attitude of
surrender and entry into a new identity in Christ. The defining
characteristic for such a person is that they are now 'clothed in

Christ'. In other words it is Christ that now characterises how that person is to be perceived.

The practical application of this principle was, and is, that the world is no longer to be seen through the same eyes. Paul talks of three ways in which human society was then categorised. Jew and Greek (gentile) suggested a previous way of dividing the world on religious and racial grounds between those who were Jews and those who were not. The world of that time was also divided on social and economic grounds, namely between those who were slaves and those who were not. Finally he noted division on the basis of gender. Paul was clear in what he was teaching. The world was no longer to be fundamentally looked at as being divided into categories defined by race, culture, economics, social class or gender.

To agree with the fundamental principle expressed in this part of Galatians is not to say that these divisions ceased to exist in society at large. However, if a person became a Christian their most fundamental identity was Jesus Christ above and beyond anything else. In a world still consumed with identity based on race, culture, economics and gender this is a fundamental teaching for any Christian church, including the Church of Ireland, to embrace. No matter what claims anyone may place upon the identity of the Church of Ireland, as a Christian church the essence of its identity is Jesus Christ rather than anything that is based on culture, race, history, social class or economic background. Such a principle has profound implications in any society consumed with identity.

2. Focus

There are many things that compete for the finite supply of energy and zeal in a human being. Christians are not exempt from this competition for passion. Detail of this may differ for Christians in twenty-first century society, but the same conflicts have existed as long as fallible human nature has. Amongst all the competing drains on our passion, what has first claim?

The Bible is very explicit in this regard. Christ has a clear in-

junction for each and every disciple. Each Christian must seek
first the kingdom of God. The word kingdom is one not readily
used in everyday contexts today. It literally denotes a geographical area that is under the control of a sovereign, and which is
subject to their rule. When one thinks of the kingdom of God
what comes to mind is not a literal geographical area that is subject to God's rule. It is actually to think beyond this. The kingdom of God is any area of human life, whether corporate or individual, where the rule or reign of God exists. To limit this to
physical or geographical area is much too limiting. The kingdom, or rule, of God can be expressed in tangible physical behaviour but also in terms of attitude of mind and heart. To overly
elaborate this is to obscure the principle. There must not be anything or anyone that commands greater passion or commitment
on the part of any Christian believer. Those things that compete
will range from the banal and domestic to the greater human
passions and ambitions. The same principle holds nevertheless.
The first priority of any Christian is to actively look for the kingdom of God to be manifested in their lives. It is not to say that
there are not other passions or ambitions in the life of the
Christian. It is to say that where these compete, obscure or conflict with the values of the Kingdom of God there is no question
of priority. As for an individual so for a church.

To define principle is one of the easiest things in the world.
To actually work out the implications in ordinary life contexts is
where the pain and challenge more often come. The principles
elaborated thus far would seem to be foundational to the identity
of any Christian church, including the Church of Ireland. To this
we add two further things that are at the very essence of what it
means to be a Christian church.

3. Neighbours with history

If only it were possible to find some part of the Bible that neatly
distilled the essence of Christian teaching! There is certainly one
place where Christ declared that the law and the prophets were
summed up and the essence of scripture distilled. When an ex-

pert in the law asked what was required to eternal life he found that Jesus gave the essential requirement:

> Love the Lord your God with all your heart and with all your soul and with all your strength and with all your mind; and, love your neighbour as yourself.[37]

Jesus' commentary on this is 'Do this and you shall live.' Love for God was something to encompass all aspects of a human being. It was to be more than an assent of the mind, rather a total devotion. A reading of this passage reveals that there is a question within a question. Love of God was one thing, but what exactly did love of neighbour mean? More specifically, who was to be counted as a neighbour. Into this context Jesus tells the story of the Good Samaritan.

Jews and Samaritans had a history. One could look back over centuries to see how a division between these two peoples arose. The fault lines of disagreement could be traced along those of racial purity, doctrinal disputes and a long historical sense of betrayal. Strangely familiar perhaps! Jews regarded Samaritans as people to be despised and distrusted. In the light of this reality the clear principle in the parable of the Good Samaritan is startling. Core to the scripture was the commandment to love your neighbour as yourself. As to who may be included in the category of neighbour is not left to ambiguity. Jesus declares that the Samaritan, hated enemy of the Jew, was a neighbour. The principle of Christian faith is simple. Love for God is something that is meant to encompass every part of a person's being. Integral to wholehearted love for God is love for one's neighbour and the fact that this love is expressed in practice rather than mere words. An enemy thus becomes every bit as much a neighbour as a friend. Doctrine, race or history do not alter or produce exception to this. The contrary is rather the case. The Sub Committee on Sectarianism that reported to the General Synod in 1999 expressed something of this as it stated:

> The primary teaching of Jesus' life then and indeed the subject of some of his profoundest teaching is love.[39]

So far we have made the point that the Church of Ireland, because it is a Christian church, finds its most essential identity in
the person and character of Jesus Christ. This sense of identity
supersedes identity found in race, gender, social or economic
class. Its priority is to seek the kingdom or rule of God before
anything else. Devotion to God is to be something that whole-
heartedly encompasses every dimension of the person. Integral
to this commitment is the requirement to love one's neighbour.
If this meant that Jews were to view Samaritans as their neighbour then differences of race, culture, history, religion or suspicion do not exclude anyone from this category.

4. Mission

There is one further tenet that needs to be usefully added at this
point. This may be most succinctly expressed in the word mission. It was a former Archbishop of Canterbury[40] who is reputed
to have said that the church is one of the only organisations in
the world that exists for the benefit of those who are not its
members.

To attempt to give a definition to the concept of mission is to
risk limiting the all-encompassing nature of it. It is reasonable to
place significance on the parting words of Jesus to his disciples.
Matthew's gospel expresses it in these words

Therefore go and make disciples of all nations, baptising
them in the name of the Father and of the Son and of the Holy
Spirit, and teaching them to obey everything I have com-
manded you.[41]

Bishop Darling, in his eve of Synod Address in 1993, commented on the mission of the church:

What is the church's mission today? Is it not to bring men
and women into a true and real relationship with Jesus
Christ?

It is recognised that different parts of the Christian church
vary in terms of emphases and expression of mission. Rather
than seek to define how mission needs to be manifestly ex-

pressed, thus doubtless stirring polemic, it would be more useful to answer a different question entirely. To whom ought mission, however manifested, be directed? The answer to this is surely simplicity in the extreme. It is to be manifested wherever there is need. Jesus did not set boundaries in his parting words to the disciples as detailed in the Book of Acts:

> ... you shall be my witnesses in Jerusalem, and in all Judea and Samaria, and to the ends of the earth.[42]

The call to mission did not exclude the home region of the disciples. With echoes of the parable of the Good Samaritan it would also include the land associated with one's enemy. Geography, history or place excluded no one from mission. There were to be no boundaries beyond which mission could go. The responsibility for the Church of Ireland in all of this is no different from that of any other part of the Christian church. It is to offer expression and witness to the person of Christ to all, using whatever means are in accord with its own nature and calling.

Anglicanism

In the context of all that has previously been noted regarding fundamental tenets of the Christian church, we now reflect on the particular tradition of the Church of Ireland. The Church of Ireland is a member of the worldwide Anglican Communion. As implied by its name the Church of Ireland is not bound by the national boundaries in Ireland, but rather encompasses the whole island. Several dioceses actually straddle the border and include parishes in both jurisdictions. Charles Kenny describes the Church of Ireland as being

> ... a people of a particular tradition trying to lead Christian lives in Ireland today.[43]

The Church of Ireland, in common with the rest of the Anglican Church, has episcopacy. This means that Ireland is divided into a number of large geographical areas known as dioceses, some of which straddle the border. A diocese is further divided into parishes. These smaller geographical areas are overseen by a rector, whilst a diocese is led by a bishop. Each diocese has a synod that meets on an annual basis. This is a forum consisting of all licensed diocesan clergy, elected representatives from each parish, and chaired by the bishop. The ultimate legislative body of the Church of Ireland, however, is the General Synod, which meets on an annual basis. This national body consists of the House of Bishops, and a set number of clergy and parishioners elected from each diocese.

As the Church of Ireland is based on a parochial system, there is a presumption that every person living within the confines of a parochial boundary who has been baptised in the Church of Ireland is a member of that particular parish. This does not presume that every one of these individuals will be an active churchgoer. Nor does it make presumptions about their personal Christian commitment or otherwise. What it does mean is that there is a sense in which these individuals are counted as being parishioners unless they make it known otherwise. In that sense a Church of Ireland is not a gathered church, as in a group of people coming together to be part of a church where faith and commitment are the determining factors, as opposed to the vagaries of geographical boundaries.

In a parochial situation the rector, under the authority of the bishop, has ultimate responsibility for the spiritual direction of that parish, as well as the ordering of public worship. Each parish will have a Select Vestry. This is a body elected from amongst registered parishioners and also contains churchwardens, who are appointed by a rector. The formal remit of a Select Vestry is often described as being finance, furniture and fabric. Whatever may be informal practice in local situations, a Select Vestry has, with slight exception, no formal responsibility or power with regard to public worship or the spiritual direction of a parish.

It may be concluded that a rector of a parish has a large amount of autonomy even from the bishop or synod. As long as a rector obeys the rules of the Church of Ireland as laid down in the Thirty-Nine Articles, the Book of Common Prayer, and the Church of Ireland Constitution, there is considerable freedom of action. In these circumstances a bishop or synod is severely limited in its powers to intervene, unless specific rules or formularies are being clearly contravened.

Attempting to define Anglicanism is notoriously difficult. The people finding most difficulty in this regard are often Anglicans themselves. Within any Anglican Province, no less so in Ireland than anywhere else, there will be wide divergence of views and practice in many things. However, there are certain fundamental characteristics that enable Anglicanism to encompass a variety of people.

One may get a flavour of what Anglicanism is by turning to the Thirty-Nine Articles of Religion. The purposes of these, as noted in the Book of Common Prayer, are:

... for avoiding of the diversities of opinions, and for the establishing of consent touching true religion.[44]

These Articles of Religion, along with what is found in the Book of Common Prayer, are a summation of traditional Church of Ireland doctrinal teaching. In determining a course on any matter Anglicanism uses three strands in any such exploration: scripture, tradition and reason.

Anglicanism seeks to be simultaneously catholic and reformed in nature. These two aspects of the historic Christian faith are sometimes portrayed as being incompatible. Anglicanism does not believe this to be so, but rather seeks to act as a bridge between the two. In regard to this Dr Alan Acheson describes the Church of Ireland as embodying the strands of:

evangelical assurance, catholic piety and reformed doctrine.[45]

Using the term 'ecumenical' is often tantamount to producing a red rag to a bull. The concept of ecumenism is often derided without sufficient attention being given to what protagonists actually mean when using the word. As with most other issues within the Church of Ireland, there is a wide variety of views on this matter. The Anglican Communion is firmly committed to the concept of ecumenism in the form of constructive dialogue and agreement with other churches where possible. The Church of Ireland shares this commitment. Illustrative of this is the dialogue taking place with the Methodist Church at present. Commitment to ecumenism also encompasses dialogue with the Roman Catholic Church. A prominent Church of Ireland bishop, Archbishop McAdoo, was a co-chairman of the body that produced the ARCIC Reports covering various key aspects of dialogue between the Anglican and Roman Catholic Church. Whilst not every member of the Church of Ireland will hold identical views with regard to ecumenism, particularly towards the Roman Catholic Church, it is clear that the church is fundamentally sympathetic to ecumenism.

To state that the fundamental character of the Church of Ireland is that of a Christian church is to desire if not deliver perfection. Having reflected upon the ideal must bring with it the recognition that 'we see through a glass darkly' ... or put more colloquially ... all is never as it should be!

This church is an all-Ireland body. However, the character varies considerably from north to south. In Northern Ireland the church has had to deal with the trauma that the last thirty years of the Troubles have brought. It has had a significant contribution to make in its pastoral care, but what of the prophetic dimension to ministry? One may describe a prophetic ministry as a desire to speak God's word into particular situations and circumstances. In a community where it is all too easy to claim God is on our side, this ministry comes fraught with possible pitfalls. Yet there is a sense that the Church of Ireland has appeared to keep its head down on the greater issues such as sectarianism that have given oxygen to the conflict and resulting violence.

There is a perception in some quarters of a close identification in the north between the Church of Ireland and unionism. This was a view given by more than one interviewee. David Quinn commented that there was a sense that the church was more hard-line in the north, and talked of:

(an) overwhelming perception of a strong political aspect because of a perceived link with the Orange Order.[46]

Others suggested that this perception was aided by a range of things from the flying of union flags from churches at particular times of the year to Archbishop Eames accepting a peerage to sit in the House of Lords.

In the Republic, the Church of Ireland has at times been rather unkindly referred to as the *Irish Times* at prayer. Behind this quip is the implication that the church here wants to be seen as liberal and with a strong personal autonomy ethic. The Republic is undergoing a profound transformation in both social and religious dimensions, with a strong tide of secularism overtaking the society. In this atmosphere the supposed 'tolerance' of the Church of Ireland is viewed as attractive, especially to urban 'post-Catholics'.

The divergence of personality between north and south is not merely cultural. It is most starkly fuelled by the crisis at Drumcree. One detects a strong sense of embarrassment as much as anything else amongst the southern Church of Ireland community. There is incomprehension as to how such a situation, so intimately yet publicly associated with a Church of Ireland church, could be allowed to continue. In the north there is a sense that there is lack of empathy in the southern community for the wider context in which this dispute is being played out.

Can a church be considered in isolation from the community that it serves? To frame a question in such a way suggests a certain tribal view of church. It is to perceive it as being little more than the badge or representative for a particular community. One must go back to the foundational principles already reflected on. The essence and identity of any church is rooted in the person of Jesus Christ. That is where all consideration must begin. To begin otherwise is to condemn a church to being the servant of a particular community rather than of Christ himself.

Robert McCarthy well expressed one of the fundamental challenges for the Church of Ireland. In considering the various structures of the church, he clarified the key question:

... how far do they assist the expansion of the gospel of

Christ, how far do they contribute to the extensions of the kingdom?[47]

This is merely an elaboration of Jesus' exhortation to seek first the kingdom of God. The challenge for the Church of Ireland in the midst of a painful and complex situation is simple. The implications of faithfulness to this simplicity are rather more complex.

CHAPTER FOUR

The Order and the Church Today

The Church of Ireland and the Orange Order are two separate organisations with no formal or official link between them. Any relationship that does exist has two strands. On the one level there is a relationship that is worked out informally in numbers of parishes throughout Northern Ireland. The other strand of relationship is the history of interweaving of interests in the past.

Examining various ways in which this is worked out will clarify what is meant by an informal relationship between the two organisations. The most obvious aspect of this is the fact that there is a large overlap in membership between the two organisations. Rectors of a number of parishes will find that a proportion of men, and some women, in a congregation also belong to the Orange Order. This is much more so the case in rural parishes, especially as one travels further west in the province. It will also be the case that members of the Order who are parishioners are often active in parish life and may be members of the Select Vestry. The fact that members of the Order are often active parishioners must not predetermine one's view of what an appropriate relationship between the two is, but it does suggest rigour in arriving at it.

It is a reality that overlap in membership also includes some members of the clergy. Although more common in the past, a number of Church of Ireland clergy are still members of the Orange Order. This will be seen in a public way at Orange parades where clergy parade wearing both clerical collar and Orange regalia. If religious services are held at such occasions, members of the clergy are often called to conduct them. It is usually the case that clergy who are members of the Order will be asked to act as chaplains in their own local lodge. It may also be that they are invited to act as chaplains at the level of Grand Lodge.

An informal relationship between Order and church may also exist in the sharing of premises. Parishes do not always have their own halls. In these situations parish activities may take place in the Orange Hall on a regular basis. Although the hall will belong to the Order it may be used de facto as a parish hall. The reverse is also the case on occasion. A local Orange lodge may not always have its own hall to conduct lodge meetings or activities. If this is so it may be that they will have permission to use a local parish hall.

The more public expression of an informal relationship is the holding of Orange services in parish churches at certain times of the year. It is often the tradition that a lodge will hold a church service on the Sunday immediately before the Twelfth of July. Such services may take place during the normal time of a church service. If members of a lodge attend a service that coincides with the normal time of parish worship, clergy will sometimes contend that this does not mean that it is an Orange service, but rather that members of the lodge are merely attending normal parish worship. Although arguable, it does seem something of an exercise in semantics as there are a number of obvious factors to distinguish it from an ordinary service.

On such occasions the lodge will parade in full regalia to and from the church service. A local band will usually lead the parade, with colours recognised by the Institution, the national flag and other standards often being carried. These will usually be carried into the church and placed at the front, near the Communion Table for the duration of the service. The normal service as would be used by the parish on that day may be conducted, with the members of the lodge attending in full regalia. It is sometimes the case that a special Order of Service is used but this will most often closely resemble a Book of Common Prayer service. Officers of the attending lodge may read the lessons at such services and will usually ask for an opportunity to say a few words of thanks to the local Rector for his or her co-operation in the holding of the service. It is often the case that the local lodge will make a request for a special preacher. This will usually be a member of the Church of Ireland clergy who also happens to be in the Orange Order. It is often the local tradition that any collection made in the service will be given either in total or in part to an Orange charity. Generally the congregation at the end of the service sings the National Anthem. Whatever one's view, it is hard to argue that such an occasion is no more than normal parish worship, merely distinguished by the fact that members of the lodge happen to be attending.

There are other occasions when an Orange lodge may request a special service. The format for these will be broadly similar to that noted above, and will usually be for such events as the coming together of lodges in a district for a service, or to commemorate a particular event such as the Battle of the Somme. These services will be at times other than that of normal parish worship and will only involve members of the Order their family and friends.

In the Church of Ireland the conduct of worship is a matter for the local rector. Any request for a special service, or for particular arrangements regarding a service at a normal time, is also for the consideration of the rector. Responsibility for this includes all aspects of a service. This fact is recognised by the Orange Order. It has its own guidelines for the arranging of Orange services and those laid down in the Constitution of the Church of Ireland echo these.

> The conduct of the Service is ... a matter for the Minister. This includes the Order of Service, as well as the hymns, prayers, collections etc. These must be acceptable to the Minister-in Charge, whose conscience, as well as his position in law must be respected at all times.[48]

Simple observation of Church of Ireland churches in Northern Ireland reveals that a significant number have flagpoles. The General Synod of the Church of Ireland has made its comments in 1999 with regard to the flying of flags on churches. It stated that the only flags that have express sanction are the flag of Saint Patrick and the flag of the Anglican Communion. One of the markers of an informal relationship between the Order and the Church of Ireland, as often cited by those outside these organisations, is the fact that flags are flown from the top of some churches at particular times of the year. This may be the national flag or in a few instances there will be more than one flagpole and Orange colours may be in evidence. Flags are almost always flown around the Twelfth of July. They may fly for several weeks, or sometimes longer.

One may ask why the flying of flags on a church building signifies any type of relationship with the Orange Order. It is extremely rare that any other flag than the national flag or Orange colours are flown from church buildings at other times than around the beginning of July. In some instances it is reasoned that flags are flown to commemorate the Battle of the Somme, hence the timing at the beginning of July. The resonance of these battles of the First World War runs deep in the psyche of some Ulster Protestants. If this is the case then flags should only be flown around the dates associated with such commemoration. However, even the great majority of Church of Ireland members are probably unaware that this is an occasional rationale for the flying of flags.

Amongst Protestants and Catholics alike there is more likely to be the perception that the reason flags are flown is because of the Twelfth of July and the Orange demonstrations associated with it. Anything more nuanced is hardly creditable. Even if there is no formal link or relationship between the Church of Ireland and the Orange Order the sight of flags being flown from churches around the time of Orange demonstrations unambiguously sends out its own signals to affiliate and critic alike.

Common History
As with so many other aspects of life in Ireland, history does

much to mould perception of the present. Whilst one may not find a history of official links between the Church of Ireland and the Orange Order it is nevertheless true that both institutions seem to have found common cause at key times in Irish history. The Orange Order has been a visible expression of unionism. The Church of Ireland may at times have been similarly described.

Themes that now seem familiar to us in describing the dynamics of conflict may be observed prior to the Reformation in Ireland. The Anglo-Norman presence in Ireland condemned Irish culture as being

> ... so different from their own, as barbarous, with the effect that their efforts to subdue Ireland were justified in their minds as a civilising and Christianising mission.[49]

Such an attitude became received wisdom and helped characterise struggles of the time as being between good and evil. It was with the advent of the Reformation in Ireland that such conflict began to be seen as between Protestant and Catholic. Many Irish people saw the Reformation in terms of the English crown using further means to extend control and power in Ireland. It cannot in any sense be seen as a purely religious affair, but an entwining of political and economic interests with the religious.

The Church of Ireland did not escape in this regard. Dr Kenneth Milne described the impression of the Church of Ireland at that time as being 'an agent of the English conqueror'. By 1560 the Church of Ireland was the legally established state church, with penalties levied for failure to conform. Although an established church, the Church of Ireland was in numerical terms a minority one. Not only was it numerically much smaller than the Catholic population but was also widely scattered so that there was no county were it could claim to be the majority. It was a small community seemingly surrounded by a resentful Catholic population.

The Reformation in Ireland was used as an instrument for subduing the Irish. At times it was difficult to distinguish it from a process of colonisation and the brutal military campaigns that

would accompany this. Rather than being seen as gospel motivated it was rather perceived as being inspired by the state and
more to do with political control. The historian Marianne Elliot
reflected on the failure of the Reformation to take hold amongst
the Catholic Irish and laid some of the responsibility for this on
the Church of Ireland at that time. As the established church it
was the church of the ascendancy.

> Staffed predominantly with English and Scottish clerics – the
> existence of some genuinely Protestant clergy not surviving
> into a second generation – the Church of Ireland pursued a
> policy of winning the Irish from their 'stubborn traditional-
> ism and ignorant superstition' through compulsion and
> Anglicisation and simply succeeded in setting itself apart as
> elitist and foreign.[51]

The soon to be familiar theme of religion as a prime demarcation in Ireland was becoming realised. The Church of Ireland
began to develop its own doctrinal formularies and in 1615 produced the Irish Articles. This was heavily influenced by theological work that had taken place in the English church and be-
trayed an anti-Catholicism that reflected the background of
struggle in Ireland at that time. The view of the Catholic church
ranged between an acknowledgement of it as being a Christian
church, albeit extremely corrupt, and that where it was viewed
as not being a true church at all. Alan Falconer reflects on the development of theology in this regard

> ... the role of the churches ... in the situation of conflict in
> Ireland has been to reinforce the alienation of the different
> communities by developing theologies-in-opposition.[52]

As it was the established church at a time when numerically
relatively small, it seemed that membership brought privileges.
This was seen all the more starkly in the light of the Penal Laws
which the Irish parliament progressively developed from 1695.
Amongst its strongest supporters was often the Church of
Ireland. The parliament that enacted such laws was exclusively
Church of Ireland. Although the Penal Laws in Ireland did have
some express effect on church life, in that it was not until 1869

that Catholic bishops were allowed legal use of their titles, Marianne Elliot points out:

> ... the main target of the Penal Laws was property and its associated political power.[53]

The progressive effects of these laws on Catholic land rights mak e stark reading. Catholics were not allowed either to purchase land or to take a lease on land for longer than thirty-one years. Should a Protestant heiress marry a Roman Catholic she automatically lost her claim. In respect of estates owned by Catholics these had to be divided amongst male heirs except in the situation of the eldest turning Protestant. If this became the case he would thus become the sole owner, neven during the lifetime of his father.

These and other stipulations meant that Catholic landowners faced the prospect of losing their lands if they did not conform, that is to say become Protestants and raise their offspring thus. Particularly in the eighteenth century 'land conformism' amongst the Catholic population was not uncommon. Elliot details other measures within the Penal Laws that pressurised Catholics towards conformism.

> After 1693 Catholics were effectively debarred from sitting in parliament by the requirement of oaths against the Pope's deposing power and transubstantiation. But they could continue to vote if they took oaths of allegiance and abjuration, until that right was removed in 1728. Other measures debarred them from local government, the higher levels of the legal profession and from Ireland's only university.[54]

If not spoken, the rationale behind the Penal Laws was nevertheless plain. Dr Joe Liechty describes this as he reflects on the development of such legislation in the light of rebellions in the 1640s and 1680s:

> Catholics had proven themselves politically treacherous and now they must be kept weak so that they could not rebel again; it was their religion that made them rebels, so Catholicism must be eliminated, or at least tightly controlled;

land ownership was the foundation of political power, so Catholic capacity to rebel could be checked by eliminating or reducing Catholic land ownership. In this logic, the union of political, economic, and religious considerations was seamless.[55]

The Church of Ireland was inevitably going to be the 'beneficiary' of such laws. In its history it did not show itself a paragon of protest at the injustice of such regulation or as an unwilling recipient of any benefits that accrued from the structural disadvantage that Catholics remained under in the Penal Laws. A numerically weak church was surviving through its reliance on the state!

There is indeed much in the history of the church, both prior to and since disestablishment in 1869, that sees it interwoven with the greater dynamics that were taking place in Ireland. From the very beginnings the Church of Ireland was seen by many to be associated with Empire, and certainly with the Protestant Ascendancy. This would have been a perception not entirely exclusive to non-members. Dr Duncan Morrow describes historical perception of the church as:

... historically part of the power system: More interested in being part of the power system than the gospel.[56]

It could be argued that, not withstanding the faithful witness of some, the church gave the impression of defining its mission in terms of catering for the establishment. Some of its actions could certainly not be described as politically neutral. Such perception was not going to be undermined by the great debate over the Home Rule issue.

Throughout the Home Rule crisis the Church of Ireland steadfastly opposed the Home Rule Bills. As the history of that period progressed it may be noted that the Solemn League and Covenant of 1912 was signed by all but one bishop. Church of Ireland historians readily acknowledge that the church had a distinctly unionist flavour. McCarthy comments to this effect:

Throughout the first half of the twentieth century almost all leaders of the Church of Ireland were staunchly loyalist, not to say unionists.[57]

The Church of Ireland was regarded as being very much on the British side until 1922. In the Republic from that time onwards the church began to diminish in numerical terms. One has the sense of a small bewildered minority having to adapt to a state of affairs that it would not have initially chosen whilst the Roman Catholic church was very much the dominant Christian denomination. The Church of Ireland, in adapting to a new state of affairs, did not want to be accused of being disloyal to the new state. In a short period of time it had lost prestige, established position and took on a much lower profile. Perhaps permeating this early period from 1922 onwards there was insecurity bred out of fear as to whether it had the ability to survive as a church.

As the Orange Order looks back over its history it can see how its importance as a voice for unionism grew in times of perceived threat. In its history the Church of Ireland cannot distance itself from the contention that it also has been at times a voice for unionism. Recent years have seen a change in this regard, not least caused by the controversy surrounding Drumcree. As Dean David Chillingworth comments:

The Church of Ireland is moving away from being an expression of moderate unionism.[58]

Whatever the stance of the church in the present, observers within and outside both institutions may be forgiven for seeing how shared values in the past have given a historical strand to the informal relationship between the two.

It needs to be emphasised that an expressed informal relationship between the Church of Ireland and the Orange Order does not exist in every parish in Northern Ireland. There are many parishes where the presence of the Orange Order is negligible in the membership of a congregation. Neither does every parish host Orange services nor make a practice of flying flags during the month of July. It is also less common now for clergy to be members of the Orange Order.

Apart from some areas in border counties it is of no relevance to talk of a relationship between the Church of Ireland and the Orange Order in the Republic of Ireland. There are a number of Lodges in Cavan, Donegal and Monaghan that will parade at Twelfth of July demonstrations in Northern Ireland. However, for most of the Republic such a relationship is not one that has any day to day relevance. It is simply not an issue that will have to be faced on the ground by members of the clergy or congregations. Where it does become a relevant issue to parishes in the Republic is in the association of the church with the crisis that surrounds the church at Drumcree, in Armagh Diocese.

CHAPTER FIVE

To the Heart of the Matter

Shared Truth?

Differences or even outright disagreements with other churches or organisations do not necessarily rule out dialogue or relationships. However, it is not possible for the Church of Ireland to have an association with another organisation if differences of belief and practice are of a fundamental character. That is not to say that the right of that organisation to exist is disputed or that Christian civility and love should not be shown to its membership. It does mean, however, that the Church of Ireland will choose not to be associated with it. An example of this may be seen in the fact that the Church of Ireland does not dispute the civil rights of Mormonism to exist, nor would it condone anything less than Christian behaviour towards the membership of the Church of Jesus Christ of Latter Day Saints. However, the doctrinal differences between the two are of such profound nature that it would be doctrinally incompatible for any association or relationship beyond this to exist.

There are three measures to use when considering whether or not the Orange Order, or any other body for that matter, is doctrinally compatible with the Church of Ireland. One may variously ask whether or not its basic beliefs are compatible with biblical truth, Reformed faith, and the Thirty-Nine Articles of Religion. It will inevitably be the case that, due to disagreement over emphases and interpretation, there will be dispute in all three. Deciding the matter finally becomes one of degree.

The Orange Order is very explicit in the significance that it

gives to the Bible. The Institution makes great play of the fact
that it seeks to oppose biblical error but also to encourage scriptural truth. The place of the Bible as a rule of doctrine and practice is very clear within the documentation of the Orange Order.
The 'Qualifications' state that there is a responsibility on members to:

> honour and diligently study the Holy Scriptures and make
> them the rule of his faith and practice.[59]

Rather than being in any way opposed to the doctrines of
Reformed faith, the Order explicitly states that part of its very
substance is to defend and promote them. The *Basis of the
Institution* states that the Order is:

> ... composed of Protestants, united and resolved to the ut-
> most of their power to support and defend ... the Protestant
> Religion. ... It is exclusively an Association of those who are
> attached to the religion of the Reformation.[60]

The Order is openly committed to the scripture being a rule
of faith and practice, and cites attachment to Reformed religion.
An examination of the Thirty-Nine Articles of Religion does not
suggest any particular doctrinal deviance with doctrines ad-
hered to by the Order. On this basis it seems impossible to argue
that there is a doctrinal incompatibility between the Church of
Ireland and the Orange Order. In fact the opposite is true.

Shared Values?

The Orange Order has a profoundly political dimension. From
its inception in the midst of agrarian land disputes, through the
formation of the Unionist Party, and in the role it has played in
Northern Ireland politics to the present, it is not possible to
argue that this dimension has not been part of its very essence.
In its inception, history and present practice it is not a politically
neutral organisation. It very clearly stands for a particular political identity and constitutional arrangement. By friend and foe
alike it is perceived to have a political dimension. Rev Eric
Culbertson is both a member and noted apologist for the Order.

When asked about a political dimension for the Order he commented:

> Clearly the Orange Order has a political side to it... (It is)
> clearly not a politically neutral organisation ... (it would) cer-
> tainly be a unionist organisation.[61]

The Orange Order inextricably links the gospel with one
particular political and constitutional arrangement. It will be argued by some in the Order that maintaining the union with
Great Britain, as well as defending the throne under the House
of Windsor, is the arrangement most conducive for the health
and spread of the gospel in Northern Ireland. This is held to be
particularly so when considering the alternative of unity with
the Irish Republic in a state that would then be felt to be domi-
nated by the influence of the Roman Catholic Church.

One must take issue with the contention, either explicit or
implicit, that the gospel somehow needs a particular constitutional arrangement to ensure its health and future in Ireland. In
this regard there is a problem on two counts. Firstly, one disputes that there is a biblical precedent for the gospel to need a
specific constitutional arrangement to ensure its welfare. Rather,
there are grave dangers in this. Secondly, there is the danger of
too closely aligning the gospel with one particular identity, so
that commitment to one implies a necessary commitment to the
other.

It is illuminating to look back to the Old Testament, in particular to the early history of the Children of Israel as they made
their roots in the Promised Land. This followed captivity in
Egypt and forty years spent wandering in the wilderness before
entering into the Land of Canaan. In these early years of settling
into a new land the leadership of the Children of Israel was provided by a succession of wise individuals known as Judges.
Prominent among them was the prophet Samuel.

The Children of Israel became unhappy with such a leadership arrangement. Whether through a sense of insecurity or
some other reason they began to feel the need for a more tangible form of leadership. This was particularly so as they observed

the increasing age of Samuel. Specifically they felt that their security would best be served by having a king to rule them. The biblical record in 1 Samuel 8 recounts how the people continually asked for a king. It is clear from the record that such a desired arrangement was contrary to the divine plan. The Children of Israel had had to depend on God for their deliverance from Egypt, guidance through the wilderness, establishment in the Land of Canaan, and all under a succession of leadership. The danger appeared to be that once the people had the leadership of a king there would be a temptation to place their most profound trust for the future in such a figurehead and 'constitutional arrangement' rather than an active dependency on God.

Desiring a particular political arrangement is legitimate. To move a step further than this and somehow link the health of the gospel with a political identity is something that no part of the Christian church should countenance. If the welfare of the gospel requires a particularly conducive political arrangement one wonders why the Christian church and the cause of the gospel have made such burgeoning progress in locations where circumstances seem anything but constitutionally advantageous. One might also question whether seemingly advantageous political arrangements, such as the Constantinian Settlement, making Christianity the official religion of the Roman Empire, are always in the best long term interests of a dynamic expression of the gospel. Which political settlement is most conducive for the welfare of the gospel is most probably a fruitless and endless argument. To make one particular arrangement, whatever that may be, intimately entwined with the wellbeing of the gospel is highly questionable. In the political realities of Ireland and the rest of Western Europe, it is unsustainable.

No Christian church should be so closely identified with one particular political identity. Unfortunately, the history of the Church of Ireland has been anything but flawless in this regard. Prior to disestablishment, it was in very many ways the church of the establishment in Ireland. Its history since then has been that it has seemed at times to act as the religious dimension of one political community. Nevertheless, the close identification that the Orange Order makes between the Christian faith and a specific political identity causes a significant problem for the Church of Ireland. If it is closely identified with the Order it is by implication being closely identified with a certain political commitment. The political identity in question is valid and legitimate for any particular member of the church to subscribe to. For a the church to do so is another matter entirely.

Underneath this question of the link between the gospel and preserving the union with Great Britain is the contention that it is for the cause of Christ. There is the nagging feeling that the reality may be more to do with a defence of cultural and political Protestantism. Both these aspects of Protestantism are legitimate. What is to be resisted is the mixing of this with the cause of the gospel.

Sectarianism

Familiarity may not always breed contempt. Neither does it guarantee fullness of understanding. What is ironic in the divisions of our community is that sectarianism is not only a useful term to describe present ills but also the verbal equivalent of mud to be thrown at our enemies. The word becomes not only a source of illumination but also a useful weapon against our enemy. What better way to denigrate the reputation of our opponent than to label him or her as being ... sectarian.

The term 'sectarian' requires some definition. Cecilia Clegg and Joe Liechty describe it as being:

... a complex of attitudes, actions, beliefs and structures
 : at personal, communal and institutional levels
 : which always involves religion, and typically involves a negative mixing of religion and politics.

... which arises as a distorted expression of positive human needs especially for belonging, identity and the free expression of difference.

... and is expressed in destructive patterns of relating
 : hardening the boundaries between groups

: overlooking others

: belittling, dehumanising or demonising others

: justifying or collaborating in the domination of others

: physically or verbally intimidating or attacking others.[62]

Sectarianism will certainly include religion, but as often as not it will be characterised by a disturbing and negative mixing with politics as well. An immediate reaction in this instance would be to question whether all mixing of politics and religion is negative or helps to augment sectarianism. There are many situations where one can identify a positive contribution that religion has made to politics without contributing to a sectarian atmosphere. One example of this is the contribution of Archbishop Tutu in South Africa where he sought to apply the principles of Christian faith into the divided society in South Africa. Liechty and Clegg clarify what constitutes a negative mixing of politics and religion, where:

... religious and political factors overtly or subtly interwoven become the primary basis on which people react destructively towards other groups and individuals.[63]

Sectarianism takes place in the hearts and minds of individuals as well as in the institutions and structures in a society. As well as being expressed in words it may be present as much in attitudes. Sectarianism may not only be a tangible reality in action but also in omission. To use the definition of sectarianism as presented means not only looking at the intentions of another individual, group, or ourselves. It is also to examine the consequences of attitudes, words, actions and omission. Put most simply, if our intention in a particular set of circumstances or relationships was not intended to be sectarian but the outcome augments a destructive pattern of behaving, then we may be guilty of sectarianism.

Is sectarianism a serious sin? Whether it is or not, is the Orange Order any more liable to be guilty of it than any other exclusive organisation such as the Mothers Union, the Presbyterian Woman's Association, the Legion of Mary or the

GAA? A point made by Liechty and Clegg is that every person has a legitimate human need to be accepted, respected and to have a sense of their own identity. To have this, or to aspire to it, is not automatically to become guilty of sectarianism. Nor should it be supposed that because one has profound disagreement with another that one is guilty of sectarianism. To be different from another or to disagree with them is legitimate and valid. What identifies an action, attitude, belief or structure as being sectarian is where the aspiration for legitimate human needs becomes distorted in some way and then issues in ways of relating to others persons or groups that are destructive.

It has been clearly seen that the Orange Order has both a political and a religious dimension to it. The religious dimension of Reformed Protestant faith is accompanied by an equally focused desire to maintain a unionist settlement. A clear emphasis on religious faith is interwoven with commitment to a very particular political arrangement and aspiration. It is not the case that these are two completely separate aspects of the Order. It is rather that one dimension intimately informs and reinforces the other. The danger in such an intimate interweaving of religion and politics is the implicit belief that 'God is on our side'. To move from making a political aspiration into something indistinguishable from an article of faith, it is a short journey to the impression of divine sanction either for us or, more dangerously, against our enemy.

The image that permeates much of the ritual and ceremony of the Orange Order is that of an identity that has been forged in what may be described as 'identity in opposition'.[64] There is the clear picture of God's Chosen Few being surrounded by an inhospitable enemy. This image of Orangeism and, by implication, the Protestant population, being set over against Roman Catholics as a separate and implicitly hostile community is retold and reinforced by varieties of imagery, motifs and stories.

The picture of a Protestant community uneasily and defensively co-existing with Roman Catholics is told in two ways. There is a selective and simplistic version of history constantly

retold in ritual and story. It is the retelling of stories of siege, betrayal, deliverance from the hostile enemy, that are taken from
the previous four hundred years of history. Prominent in all of
this is obviously the rudimentary recital of the events of the
Boyne and the Siege of Derry. It is a retelling of a version of history
that is not only meant for description of the past but for the pro-
vision of an understanding of the present.

Added to a suspect rendering of history is the use of a number of biblical texts that provide motifs for the telling of
Protestant history. The appropriateness of using such texts in
this way is highly questionable. Every community has its history.
It is appropriate for each to have a story so that it can understand its past and have some perception of the present.
However, the intertwining of a particular version of history with
the appearance of selective biblical support has a number of not
only negative but also potentially dangerous outcomes.

The retelling of the story, with biblical imperatives, perpetuates a number of myths in the Protestant psyche. These have to
do with perception of others who are different from ourselves,
retelling what they have done to us in the past, and implying
their intentions not only in the present but also the future. In this
version of the story, Protestantism never sees itself as the aggres-
sive element but rather always on the defensive. This helps to
foster something essentially passive and reactive. This telling of
the story in a way that never sees Protestantism as the aggressor
brings the strong implication of Protestant innocence. Public
demonstration thus becomes, amongst other things, a celebration of innocence in the face of threat.

The culture that is encouraged by such telling of history and
application of the Bible is one that is founded on a relationship
with others that is essentially defensive. When one talks of 'others'
one is not talking in a vague sense. The defensiveness in the
story was and is against Roman Catholicism. Duncan Morrow
describes what is being perpetuated as the illusion:

> (that) Protestant security in Ireland lies in defence against the
> Roman Catholic community in Ireland.[65]

Retelling the past is a way of describing the present. Themes of threat and siege are prominent in Orangeism. There is a sense in which the Orange Order thus sees itself as an Institution called to defend its own community against serious threat. When one identifies one's community as being under threat there is a need to identify the source of the threat. There is an inevitable danger of thus imputing to the other community what Liechty and Clegg describe as a 'dangerous wrong headedness'.[66] It is a journey easily taken to fight against the threat from one's enemy, or at the very least to give a rationale as to why others would do thus.

Mixing of religion and politics in the telling of a story that celebrates and perpetuates the innocence of one community over against another, and in a way that has resonance for the present as well as the past, will hardly diminish community boundaries. It is essentially the theologisation of a political context, and is done in a way that perpetuates the myth that Protestant security is dependent on separation from and protection against Roman Catholics on the island of Ireland. It is this aspect of Orangeism that is profoundly sectarian and one that the Church of Ireland cannot be in agreement with or identify with.

Competing Passions?

There is nothing unChristian about love for one's country. Whether in Northern Ireland or the Republic of Ireland, to desire to be loyal to one's nation is not a sin or something to be ashamed of. Both unionism and nationalism in their broadest sense are legitimate and valid aspirations. A key question for an Institution that so closely entwines defence of faith and a particular political arrangement is which of these two is most important?

Sometimes we do not realise what is important to us until that thing is threatened or we face the prospect of losing it. The challenging thing about Jesus' teaching is that it is often so simple. He had his ways to get to the reality of a person's heart. A rich man comes to Jesus because he wants to find eternal life. With his ability to see the unseen, Jesus shows him a way to find it. He must give away all his possessions to the poor and then follow Jesus. This man, genuine in his spiritual search, finds that Jesus has reached the nub of the issue. Possessions were dearer to the man than his desire to follow Jesus.

It is not necessarily a sin to have wealth. It becomes a sin when possession of it becomes more important than allegiance to Christ. Sometimes we only find what place something has in our hearts when it is threatened. David Quinn posed a hypothetical question:

> If Protestants were told that they could reach more and more Roman Catholic people for the gospel if they gave up the union ... what would be their reaction?[68]

Love for country and political aspiration is legitimate. What Jesus asked of the rich young man was not something he asked of everyone. He did so in this case because he needed to see what was most important for the man in his spiritual search. Whether or not such a hypothesis as David Quinn suggests could or should become a reality is not at all the issue. What reaction is provoked provides the key to revealing priorities. With the strands of faith and politics being woven together in the Order it is a question that it must face. Which is more important, God or country? Bearing in mind that the Orange Order embodies a number of dimensions, the question is raised: is the Institution about the Christian faith or politics by other means, is the Order about gospel or country?

Politics and public life are not dirty words. It has too often been the case that Christians have compartmentalised sacred and secular, spiritual and material. It is not sinful for Christians to be involved in politics or public life. Quite the opposite! It is appropriate that Christians not only get involved in political and public life but that the church should encourage informed debate on political issues. It should take encouragement from the fact that members have opinions and are willing to argue strongly for them. It is no more politically correct for these views to be nationalist rather than unionist. What is at issue is not having political views. Neither is it the fact that these views may happen to be unionist. The question remains, which is more important: God or country? If passion for politics and country rises to such a point that it overtakes passion for Christ then it has become an idol and thus something that no church can legitimise.

Mission beyond Boundaries?

Modelled in Jesus' life is obedience to the will of his Father and the calling placed on him. His life and ministry are characterised by a willingness to listen to and obey the voice of the Father. Ultimately it was to be expressed in his willingness to walk the way of the Cross, both in Gethsemane and Calvary. It was in these places that he most clearly placed his own rights, wishes, convenience, welfare and wellbeing as secondary to his Father's will.

The responsibility for churches, and the individuals in them, to emulate the model of Jesus in submission to the Father's will. As has been noted, part of such faithfulness to the witness of the gospel requires a willingness to make its message known to all. It appears that there is nothing that the apostle Paul is not willing to do or to sacrifice in order effectively to discharge his mission. A reading of 1 Corinthians 9:19-24 amply illustrates this. Despite being a man of impeccable Jewish background and upbringing, it appears that he is willing to hold all of this lightly. His words speak for themselves:

> Though I am free and belong to no man, I make myself a slave to everyone, to win as many as possible. To the Jews I became like a Jew, to win the Jews ...To those not having the law (Gentiles) I became like one not having the law, so as to win those not having the law ... I have become all thing to all men so that by all possible means I might save some.[69]

The implications of what Paul is willing to do are as clear as they are shocking. He is willing to trade pride, power and the perception of purity in his desire to be faithful. It is an illustration of an earlier point. Any Christian church is called to communicate the truth of the gospel message to all and sundry. Samaritans, Jews, and those living at the ends of the earth were included in those needing to hear. In the New Testament there are no boundaries for mission.

There is a pastoral responsibility on the Church of Ireland as a church to care for the needs of its own membership. However, there is equally a responsibility to mission that is not restricted by boundaries. The church's responsibility is to preach the gospel to its membership, to members of the Orange Order, or to those who disagree with the Order in principle. The list is endless.

Roman Catholics and nationalists are no more or less deserving of hearing about the good news of Christ than Protestants or unionists. If one carries this argument to its logical conclusion, then one must consider the fact that forty five percent of the population in Northern Ireland come from a Roman Catholic background and are also nationalist. A crucial question for the Church of Ireland is this: in the light of the biblical principles enunciated with regard to mission, does a relationship with an organisation that has one specific and clear political dimension to its identity create boundaries that help or heed mission?

Mission is unarguably at the core of New Testament Christianity. The Church of Ireland may be comfortable with the fact that mission is implicit in the life of a church. It is sometimes very uncomfortable with defining that term in a way that will produce tangible action. It is at such a point that the debate can produce polarisation between the various theological viewpoints in the church. If the Church of Ireland is to consider whether or not a particular relationship will help or hinder its call to mission, it surely needs to have some tangible sense of what the word mission means. It will consequently need to consider whether or not there are boundaries that will define where and to whom such mission is directed. To fail to answer these questions is to risk not so much polarisation as paralysis of inaction.

Being Good Neighbours?
It is always dangerous to suggest that a particular element of Christian faith is key. What is of crucial value to one person may

seem peripheral to another. This is especially so in some of the religious debate in Northern Ireland. As has been noted before, what cannot be disputed is the fact that love for one's neighbour is a core part of authentic Christian faith. Jesus is very clear on this matter in his preamble to the story of the Good Samaritan.[70] An expert in the Jewish Law had asked what had to be done to inherit eternal life. Jesus agreed with the expert when he distilled the Law into love for God with heart, soul, mind, and strength with the injunction to love your neighbour as yourself. 'Do this and you shall live.'[71] is his commentary. The principle is clear: love for neighbour is core to authentic Christian faith.

The expert in the Law had a good question for Jesus: 'Who is my neighbour?'[72] In telling the story of the Good Samaritan Jesus was making the point that there is no one who falls outside the definition of neighbour. The expert in the Law acknowledged that the Samaritan ended up being the neighbour in the parable. This being the case, if one's enemy was one's neighbour then everyone is one's neighbour. Jesus was making the point that there are no boundaries in defining a neighbour.

To love your neighbour is such a high sounding principle that there is a danger that it may remain intangible. In the story of the Good Samaritan Jesus provides a commentary on what it might actually involve. In being a neighbour what is it that the Samaritan actually does? He places his own welfare and safety at risk by being willing to stop his journey to check on the injured traveller. If he becomes aware of the racial and religious extraction of the injured traveller he is willing to cross his own boundaries of history and disagreement to reach the unfortunate victim.

The Samaritan traveller is not so much willing to pray for the welfare of the other, but rather pay for it out of his own resources. He is the one who binds the wounds and gets off his donkey to allow the other to ride it. It is the Samaritan who spends his own time and bears the cost from his own resources to pay for the welfare of someone who ought to be his enemy. The implications of these actions do not need further elucidation. All of Jesus' teaching about loving your enemy, blessing

those who curse you and praying for those who ill-treat you,
find their greatest commentary in this story.

How might a neighbour be defined for a member of the
Church of Ireland at the beginning of a new millennium? The
answer is simple. There are simply no boundaries in Jesus'
teaching. It includes friend and foe alike. Racial, doctrinal or
historical divisions do not set new boundaries as to who is or is
not a neighbour. A neighbour is one's best friend sitting in the
pew on a Sunday morning or the friend who happens to attend a
Catholic church on Sundays. It is the person of unionist persuasion as well as the avowed nationalist. A member of Sinn Féin is
no less one's neighbour than a member of the Progressive
Unionist Party. A neighbour for a Church of Ireland parishioner
sitting in the pew of a Dublin church will include the protesting
Orangeman sitting outside the gates of Drumcree parish church
on the Sunday morning before the Twelfth of July. An Orangeman will find that his neighbour includes the people who call
most loudly for parades to be re-routed or banned.

Christian witness which has integrity in Northern Ireland
must be expressed in love for one's neighbour even, or indeed
especially, when that neighbour may also fall into the category
of political enemy or one that we may have profound doctrinal
difference with. As the Church of Ireland considers an appropriate relationship with the Orange Order, it must take into consideration how such will impact on its ability to practice love for its
neighbours.

Community Relations

Whilst being a buzzword and producing a veritable industry of
its own, community relations are nevertheless a vital aspect of
life in Northern Ireland. As a divided community it is clear that
conflict is sometimes fought with the viciousness of the bomb
and the bullet. At other times the arena will be that of street politics and division over issues that mask deeper antagonisms.

The field of community relations is worked on at provincial
and local level. The quality of community relations will be seen

not only by what our News Bulletins talk about, but how communities relate in a town, village or townland. Most simply it is concern for how the different groups within a particular community are managing to live together. Is there co-operation and common cause for the good of a particular locale? What is the state of civic society in a particular place? It is to be concerned with the right to legitimate freedom of expression for all the different segments of a particular community.

As a Christian church, the Church of Ireland is concerned with the maintenance of civic society and for the promotion of good relationships within it. To be true to some of the seminal principles of Christian behaviour it will be concerned not only for itself and those of its own ilk, but also for the wider good of all parts of the community. In determining a relationship with any other body external to itself, including the Orange Order, it will be relevant to consider how such a relationship will impact on the state of community relationship. This is true not only at national level, but on a local level as well. The issue will be not so much determined by bishop or General Synod but by local rectors and parishes on the ground.

The truth is that the impact of the Orange Order on local relationships will vary from place to place. Not every parade or public manifestation of Orangeism is contentious or a cause of offence to those outside the Order. Depending on local circumstances and the history of a locality, such events are often unremarkable

Issues in using the Bible
Both the Church of Ireland and the Orange Order declare themselves to be Christian organisations. The importance that both give to the Bible is clear. It is therefore logical to presume that the Bible will be a key measure in reflecting on any relationship between the two bodies. But how is the Bible to be used?

The Bible has been used prominently in the life and politics of Northern Ireland. In one sense a Christian might take pleasure from such an aspect of community life. Yet the pleasure is not unqualified. The fault is not in the veracity of the scripture but in the ability of any fallible human being to use it with the integrity that it deserves. Put more simply: how do we read the Bible?

The problem of how to use the Bible is that it is all too possible and tempting to use the scripture as a weapon against those with whom we disagree. The theologically or politically liberal should not imagine that they are any less prone to this than someone of a more fundamentalist persuasion. It is just as tempting to want to bludgeon one's opponent with 'Love thy neighbour' as with 'Come ye out from among them'. None of us will qualify for permission to cast the first stone in this regard. However, it is not desirable that awareness of our human frailties should cause a paralysis in using the Bible so that we never dare approach it for fear of abusing it.

Not everyone in Northern Ireland is an active churchgoer. The growing atmosphere of secularisation that has overtaken other parts of the United Kingdom and the Republic of Ireland is also taking hold in Northern Ireland. No matter how dearly Christians may regard the Bible as a rule for doctrine and practice, for more and more of the population it is becoming something of an esoteric pursuit. It is not only a general atmosphere of secularism and the effects of a post-modern culture that are the culprits. The Christian church in Northern Ireland must also accept its fair share of the blame. Christians have used the Bible as a sometime vicious weapon against opponents. It has been used to provide justification for claiming God on our side. This has been accompanied by a failure to use it to critique our own side, or to speak into more than a tight range of issues concerning private morality. All have combined to demean the way in which use of the scripture is perceived by many. Whatever means have caused us to come to such a point it will be up to the church to use the Bible in this debate in a way that is not only intelligible and relevant to our community, but also has integrity.

Any Christian who has used the Bible knows that there are times when it gives great comfort and consolation, especially in times of distress. It is also an obvious guide for doctrinal truth. Such use of the Bible is not only obvious but perfectly valid. However this does not exhaust the use of the Bible by the church or individual Christians. There is also a prophetic element in the impact of the scripture. When one thinks of the prophetic dimension, images of thundering prophets in the Old Testament may come to mind. Perhaps it is the picture of Elijah the prophet confronting the prophets of Baal on Mt Carmel[74] or some such. Of course God did not use prophets of only one type or style. One might also remember the prophet Hosea. His ministry was of quite a different style. He was called to marry a woman called Gomer who unfortunately proved to be an extremely unfaithful wife, committing not only single acts of adultery but allowing herself to become a prostitute. God told Hosea that he must continually take her back as his wife, even buying her back from a life of prostitution. One can imagine the pain and humiliation that Hosea suffered. The purpose was to graphically describe to God's people the pain and distress that their rebelliousness against God was causing him. Hardly in the same style as Elijah, but no less a prophet.

This begs the question: what does it mean to be prophetic? A prophet in the Old Testament was literally God's spokesperson. To prophesy was to speak God's word into a situation. The people of the Old Testament had the Book of the Law. God used his prophets to apply the law, his word, into the life of his people. Jesus' ministry is profoundly prophetic in its application of the scripture to life situations.

These are not the days of the Old Testament. The church believes that there is nothing more to add to the canon of scripture that already exists. What therefore is meant by the prophetic element in the use of the Bible today? It is not to imply that new bits of the Bible are to be written. It is rather that as well as being a devotional tool and guide for doctrinal truth, the scripture is also to be applied to the way in which everyday life is lived. It is to allow the Bible to speak into the situations and circumstances of ordinary life. No Christian will suggest that the Lordship of

Jesus Christ has boundaries. Quite the reverse in fact! In that case there are no boundaries of our lives, either personally or communally, beyond which the Bible will not have something to say.

The Church of Ireland often prides itself on being a voice of moderation and a middle way. There is some relief in moderation when there are extremes to choose from. Yet it is possible to address any issue in such an oblique or indirect fashion that the impact of what one is trying to say is completely lost in a sea of well meaning words. This is no less true when one is trying to speak and apply scriptural truth to an everyday situation.

To use, but hopefully not abuse, the Bible in a prophetic way is to seek to apply its truths to everyday situations. This will apply not only to areas of private morality but also to community life. There is nothing that lies beyond the boundary of the Lordship of Christ. One is obliged not only to avoid using the Bible as a weapon for one's own ends, but also to avoid using it for the theological equivalent of spin. Put in other terms, a prophetic use of the Bible is not speaking merely in such generalities that everyone will agree with, causing no offence to anyone, but in the process perhaps saying little. To allow the Bible to speak prophetically is to make practical application of its teaching, including that of Jesus, to practical situations.

A short time ago it was very much in vogue for young Christians to wear a badge that had the letters WWJD on it. When asked what this signified the reply was 'What Would Jesus Do?' In its simplest and most profound form, this is the essence of a prophetic use of the Bible. It is to constantly ask the question in the midst of any situation: what would Jesus do? Devastatingly simple, but not simplistic! It is the task of the Church of Ireland to ask such a question when considering a relationship with the Orange Order. It is its responsibility in the midst of many competing voices to also seek to answer this in a way that is not so oblique as to defy analysis.

Avoiding the pitfalls of theological spin is not the only thing to avoid when using the Bible in the present debate. The Church

of Ireland must be aware of the cultural influences that surround it. Though perhaps less apparent than in other parts of
our Western culture, Northern Ireland is not immune to the influence of postmodernism. In a postmodern culture people are
less willing to blindly accept what former voices of authority
might have to say in a particular situation. It is no longer the
case that people accept a point of view merely because of who
voices it. Whatever views the Church of Ireland voices on this
issue, and however it uses the Bible, it will have to be communicated into a culture that will not necessarily listen just because it
says so.

Perhaps of more relevance to the culture in which the Church
of Ireland must consider this relationship, and apply scriptural
truth to it, is the Ulster Protestant psyche. Ruth Dudley-
Edwards characterises it as having a 'frontiers aspect' to it. She
describes it as being that which is produced by siege. It is okay if
left alone but if not there is the 'ferocity of self-defence'.[75]
Whatever one may make of this there is certainly a sense in
which the Ulster Protestant mentality does not like being told
what to do. With a strong element of determination and indeed
stubbornness in it, 'handing something down from on high', albeit in an attempt to apply biblical truth to a relationship, may
not be the most effective means of approaching the matter.

One interviewee described the reaction of some Orangemen
to a sermon preached at an Orange service in a Church of
Ireland church. The service had obviously taken place around
the time of disturbances at Drumcree and the preacher had
made it the subject for some of his sermon, with allusions to the
gospel injunction to 'love our neighbour'. The reaction of one
Orangeman to the sermon was 'I didn't come to hear this, I came
to hear the gospel.'

Is it seriously to be contended that any exposition or application of the Bible in other areas of life beyond a call for personal
salvation, or that does not make explicit allusion to it, is somehow an erroneous proclamation?

Resistance to the more social aspects of the gospel message is

not always because of a sense that this is somehow not the real
gospel. There is perhaps a particular resistance in the human
psyche when the social implications of following the gospel are
drawn out in such a way as to touch raw nerves, or that seem to
go against dearly held opinions.

Anti-Catholicism and Ecumenism
There is an obvious emphasis in the Orange Order on its
Protestant character. As it says of itself:

> The purpose of the Orange Order is to bring together the
> Protestants of various denominations ... into one homogen-
> eous grouping to maintain their Protestant religion and way
> of life ...[76]

As a means of maintaining and promoting Protestantism, it
declares itself in opposition to biblical error and the encouragement of scriptural truth. In its quest to promote Protestantism
and resist error it identifies Roman Catholicism as embodying
much that has to be resisted. As the Order goes back in history to
the Reformation it sees a movement having profound disagreement with key teachings and tenets within Roman Catholicism.
Such disagreement and scepticism was not merely in the arena
of religious belief. In the political and religious struggles surrounding the Reformation there was a sense of resisting a system which was detrimental to liberty. This attitude to
Catholicism in both the religious and political sphere is one that
resonates up to the present day in the psyche of Orangeism. This
is vividly illustrated in *The Qualifications of an Orangeman*:

> He should strenuously oppose the fatal errors and doctrines
> of the Church of Rome, and scrupulously avoid countenanc-
> ing (by his presence or otherwise) any act or ceremony of
> popish worship; he should by all lawful means, resist ascen-
> dancy of that church, its encroachments, and the extension of
> its power, ever abstaining from all uncharitable words, ac-
> tions or sentiments towards Roman Catholics.[77]

The deep antipathy and suspicion towards the Roman

Catholic Church is not only regarding its teachings and institutions. There is also deep suspicion as to the motives and strategies of this church in the past and present conflict in Ireland. It is clear that Orangeism has regarded Roman Catholicism as a threat to religious liberty and biblical faith. One has a sense that in the Orange psyche there is a belief that the strategy of the Roman Catholic Church is to submerge and absorb Protestants in Ireland. It is in comprehending some of this thought that one sees what may fuel and provide theological rationale for resisting a united Ireland. It is still believed that, whatever social and religious changes may have taken place in the Republic of Ireland, were Ireland to be united the Roman Catholic Church would heavily influence it. Such is the suspicion of the Roman Catholic Church as an institution that there is a belief that it would have the means and the desire within a united Ireland to control individual judgement and political power, and this to the detriment of Protestantism. In the effort to resist a united Ireland Steve Bruce describes what some Protestants believe to be at stake in the struggle between 'the preservation of Ulster and their subordination in a Roman Catholic theocracy'.[78]

Orangeism makes a theological link between the desire to resist a united Ireland at all costs and the preservation of Protestant faith. As they remember the Reformation, with its perceived requirement to preserve biblical truth and maintain vigilance against a church that they believed threatened this, there comes the requirement to resist any form of government that would be under the influence of such a church. To truly appreciate the psyche that motivates this part of Orangeism it is necessary to see that the motivating force is a mixture of the theological and political. One provides rationale and impetus for the other.

Such a theological and political worldview, that emphasises vigilance and defence against the threat that Roman Catholicism poses, has deep resonance with how some Protestants perceive the world to be, and Northern Ireland politics in particular. There is the deep suspicion that political activity and manoeuvrings are not just the result of political aspirations alone but are

part of a battle between Northern Ireland, as one of the 'last bas-
tions' of biblical Protestantism in Western Europe, and Roman
Catholicism. Although the strength of views will vary with the
individual there is a strong element within Orangeism that believes that Roman Catholicism is a religious deception. If one
then considers the reality that religious affiliation has become
identified with the conflicting communities in Northern Ireland,
it is one more strand of suspicion to add to the atmosphere of
division. It is an unfortunate fact that attitudes with regard to religion have the effect of negatively reinforcing political views.

Orangeism provides a strong and definite worldview, particularly with regard to the historic conflict in Ireland. Most religious belief will seek to give an interpretation of how the world
is. The analysis that Orangeism gives to the conflict in Ireland
means that it is very easy to see conflict as religious. If such a
conflict is profoundly religious in nature, in the sense of resistance to the influence of Roman Catholicism, then a threat can be
interpreted as a confirmation of the truth of one's religious beliefs and the falsity of that of Catholic opponents. Steve Bruce
adds his commentary to this.

> Religious conflict combined with difference in language, eth-
> nic identity, and economic circumstances have created basic
> divisions in the people who populated Ireland. Such divi-
> sions meant that the formulation of political interests would
> deepen and reinforce the religious divisions.[79]

There have been many attempts to define the nature of the
conflict in Northern Ireland. Some will emphasise the division
between British an Irish. There are others who present an analysis of the situation in starkly religious terms, in that they see it as
a religious war. With the passing of the years division between
Irish and British has often been identified as simply that between Catholic and Protestant. The psyche of Orangeism contributes to a sense in which the conflict is characterised in religious terms. Whether or not one concurs with this view there is
undoubtedly an antipathy between Catholics and Protestants
that seems to be fuelled by something additional to political de-

sires.

There is obvious doctrinal disagreement between the Orange Order and the Roman Catholic Church. However, the particular Orange rendering of history that celebrates Protestant innocence and Catholic threat, as well as the use of selective biblical texts, suggests a intellectual legitimising of anti Catholicism that at the very least reinforces ignorance, if not hatred. Such a retelling of history, with the use of biblical paradigms legitimises misinformation and reinforces images of Roman Catholicism that are highly caricatured with a strong political tincture. It is difficult to imagine how the swearing of an anti-Catholic oath and the annual celebration of Protestant victory might endear one to an individual Roman Catholic. It would be an illuminating exercise to compare the numbers of Protestants who have been actively lost to that faith by Catholicism as against those whose faith has been dimmed by materialism and secularism. It raises the suspicion that anti-Catholicism is politics by other means and that defence of Protestant religion is really defence of cultural Protestantism. Defence of cultural Protestantism is perfectly valid, as is having political aspiration. What is not is to legitimise it with anti-Catholicism.

Is the Church of Ireland an ecumenical church? Not everyone in the church will believe that it should be. There are those who will share some of the attitude that Orangeism has towards Roman Catholicism. However, the clear ethos of the Church of Ireland as a church is that it is firmly committed to ecumenism, including ecumenical dialogue with the Roman Catholic Church. An examination of the Thirty-Nine Articles of Religion witnesses to the fact that there are profound differences with Roman Catholic teaching and practice. The tone in which the Articles presents this disagreement may be more a statement of the Church of Ireland in the seventeenth century rather than today, however there is no denying the reality of the divergence. Yet the stance of the church is that, whilst it is a clear product of the Reformation and definitely remains within that tradition, it is still committed to ecumenical dialogue with Roman

Catholicism.

Whatever may be the interpretation and attitude of individuals within the Church of Ireland, the church does not sit with the particular analysis that Orangeism has of the threat of Roman Catholicism, and the tone that this brings to the present conflict. If the ethos of the Church of Ireland is ecumenical and that of the Orange Order is avowedly not then this must have an effect on defining any relationship between the two bodies.

CHAPTER SIX

Moving Beyond Analysis

An unfortunate aspect of life in Northern Ireland is that it is all too easy to demonise others with whom we have profound disagreement. We paint a caricature in our mind of a group of people with whom we disagree. What is caricatured as much as anything is the motivation of the other group. It is a refusal to take the other seriously, and to question how anyone could have particular beliefs and practices. We shudder to think who might be guilty of such a thing.

To refuse to demonise someone is not to imply that we do not disagree with him or her. If that person or group has injured us it is not to pretend that such has not happened. To refuse to demonise another person or group is not to deny the pain that may be caused by their actions. It is legitimate to present a critique of the beliefs and actions of the other group, but not at the level of ridicule and caricature. The conduct of debate on such a level adds little dignity or integrity to any of the protagonists.

A commitment to dialogue and respect of the person is due no less to members of the Order than those of other persuasions. Whether or not members of the Order are committed Christians and members of Church of Ireland parishes, there is a responsibility on those outside its ranks to refuse to demonise it. The crisis at Drumcree has done little to engender sympathy for the organisation. As a result there are many within the Protestant community in Northern Ireland who find little to identify with or espouse in terms of what they see to be its values. The Church of Ireland community in the Republic of Ireland has little sympathy and less understanding of it. Those outside the Protestant community, north and south, will feel a sense of alienation from the Order

The conflict in Northern Ireland has not stopped because the level of violence and terrorism has decreased. Other means for fighting the conflict have been developed. The aggression that causes, and is caused by, the conflict in our community finds other channels. The parades issue is a prime example of community antagonism in Northern Ireland being fought in another context, and most vividly in the crisis that threatens on an annual basis around the environs of the parish church of Drumcree.

Parades can provide a context for politics by other means for all protagonists, as well as opportunity for observers to advance their own particular agendas. Not every Orange parade is benign or passes off without remark in Northern Ireland. Yet many parades do pass off without incident or offence being given. Whatever the circumstances of any one particular parade it is implausible to suggest that elements within republicanism have not taken opportunities to capitalise and increase agitation in certain situations within the context of a greater agenda of political struggle. The Orange Order has been demonised and politically manoeuvred by various parts of the republican movement.

The Church of Ireland is a body separate from the Orange Order. Its calling is not to promote the aims and objectives of institutions that are independent of it, such as the Orange Order. The same holds true for other groups or organisations. Any action by the Church of Ireland ought to be entirely coincidental to other agendas in its calling to live out an authentic Christian witness in a complex and divided situation.

The parish church at Drumcree does more than provide a compelling photographic backdrop for an isolated conflict. As well as being symbolic of who is winning or losing in Northern Ireland, it provides a potent example of the dilemmas the Church of Ireland faces in determining an appropriate relationship with the Orange Order. It has become impossible to think of such a relationship without it being coloured by events past and present surrounding Drumcree. A relationship between these two bodies must not be determined by the circumstances of one particular situation. Nevertheless it lays down a challenge for the hierarchy, clergy and membership of the Church of Ireland to enunciate gospel issues in a complex situation that is not going to simply go away.

The temptation in any discussion of the Orange Order and the Church of Ireland is to concentrate on the situation surrounding Drumcree. The crisis is associated with an official Orange Order parade that comes immediately from Morning Worship at Drumcree parish church. There is simply no credible way of disassociating one from the other.

No one is suggesting that there are not greater political dynamics at work as well as the intricacies of a local situation. In a television news piece one BBC journalist put into words what many others have guessed but could not quite express. It was the reality that the Drumcree situation is not just about the rights and wrongs of marching down a particular piece of road. It has become loaded with so much more, as symbols easily are in Northern Ireland:

It is about who is winning and who is losing in Northern Ireland.[80]

The fact that the conflict at Drumcree has become so heavily laden with symbolism only serves to muddy the waters. In some ways it has come to resemble the famous court case in Charles Dickens' *Bleak House*. In that particular instance a court case between two parties had existed for so many years that the original antagonisms had become clouded. This did not stop it from exhausting everyone who dared to become a party to it. When eventually solved, it transpired that so vast were the resources expended in the struggle that there was nothing left even for the parties involved, with at least one party dying a broken man. Whatever the cause of the original dispute it had taken a life of its own and proceeded to consume and waste those who became party to it. That such was always going to be the case was obvious to the disinterested observer. As with conflict in any human context, the longer it goes on the higher seem the stakes, and the price of ultimate victory may seem hollow when surveying the waste in human lives, relationships and resources.

What is happening at Drumcree has become a scandal. Archbishop Eames, in an article in the *Church of Ireland Gazette* commented:

> ... the Church of Ireland cannot condone, accept or tolerate in any way the scenes we have witnessed or its name being blackened by those who have shown such rejection of its ethos and teaching. Much of what I have heard spoken at Drumcree on Sunday 9th July (2000) is very far from my understanding of the teaching of Christ, let alone the principles of the Church of Ireland.[81]

The scandal not only lies in the actions and attitudes clearly linked with that dispute but also in the atmosphere that each of us has contributed to and that allows such a focus of conflict to continue. If this is so, then the answer to the scandal is closer to home than supposed.

> ... these groupings (at Drumcree) are acting out, in a dramatic high profile way, the struggle which is raging in small and large ways throughout Northern Ireland. Their struggle is everyone's struggle, and the best way that most people can contribute to a resolution is by working on their own sectarian issues, thereby not only modelling a different way but also beginning to change the overall context within which Drumcree is taking place.[82]

Debate on the specific issues and conflicting 'rights' surrounding this particular parade can easily become a quagmire from which truth may hardly emerge. What is beyond debate is the fact that this dispute has become the scene and pretext for violence for several years. In the time that the dispute has lasted one member of the Royal Ulster Constabulary has died as a result of injuries received from a pipebomb, and two civilians have also been murdered in associated violence. Added to this are the scenes of pipebombs and missiles being thrown at members of the security forces and acts of civil disorder that paralyse

Northern Ireland on what seems like an annual basis.

There may be a genuine sense of grievance amongst many members of the Orange Order that they are not permitted to make their return parade on what they contend is their traditional route. No doubt there is a similar level of grievance on the side of those who are unhappy for the Order to take such a route. Whatever the case may be, it is difficult to conclude that the cause of the gospel and Reformed faith is done anything more than a grievous harm by these events. There is simply no credible argument to suggest that there is a gospel issue involved. Whatever the real political context may be, it gives no justification for what takes place. Nor can it be argued that the matter is defence of the gospel. If there is the suggestion that it is such, then it is a defence that the gospel could and should do without.

What the ongoing dispute at Drumcree is bringing into focus is the reality that the Church of Ireland is separating from the Orange Order. The Drumcree situation has brought the dynamics of this into the open. The reality of two organisations diverging is probably most keenly felt by members of the Church of Ireland who also happen to be in the Order. This breeds its own confusion and insecurity. Debate on a denominational level, at General Synod, and practice on parochial level is making it clearer that both organisations are independent of one another, and that neither exists for the nurture of the other. This is so whether or not members of both bodies may or may not incidentally share common culture, history and political aspiration.

A wearisome facet of history in Northern Ireland is the claim by various organisations that they are not directly associated with violence, and thus have no moral link with it. Repetition does not of itself confer truth. These claims are familiar exercises in semantics with no credibility. The Orange Order cannot credibly claim that it is free of moral association from the ugly and illegal manifestations of the Drumcree dispute. Even if this were not the case, the Order still has to explain why paramilitary bands are allowed to take part in its main Twelfth of July demonstration in Belfast, or why paramilitary paraphernalia is sold at the Field. The sight of anything that celebrates violent republican paramilitarism at a public demonstration by an organisation devoted to Catholic faith would be offensive, morally repugnant and indefensible. It is no less so when the reverse is the case?

There are all sorts of dynamics laid bare within the Church of Ireland in this crisis. It has shown the tensions that arise between members of the church north and south of the border. Particularly in the south there is a sense of outrage and scandal that such a situation linked to a Church of Ireland church is allowed to continue. Yet circumstances have shown that there is not a clear road for the Church of Ireland to walk along to resolve the matter. The situation has shown the autonomy that a rector and select vestry have in dealing with local situations. It has illustrated the limited means that a diocesan bishop or General Synod has at its disposal if there is a desire to intervene in such a situation.

For some members of the Church of Ireland the Orange Order's relationship with the Church of Ireland is a normal part of church and community life. Yet not all of the voices in this debate are in support of such a relationship with the Orange Order. There are many members of ordinary Church of Ireland parishes who are unhappy with any association. One pressure group that has come into existence within the Church of Ireland in recent years is Catalyst. This group has a very critical view of the Orange Order and the way in which the Church of Ireland relates to it. Its analysis is sceptical of the religious aspects of the Order. It regards it as being somewhat obsessed by anti-Catholicism to the point of irrational fear, and offering an analysis of Roman Catholicism that is seriously flawed. In the Order it sees something that regards the Roman Catholic Church as so powerful that it presents a version of Protestantism that is fearful and negative. What is thus promoted is something that is essentially anti something else as opposed to positively joyful. In terms of the social contribution that the Order makes, it contends that sectarian and negative effects of its activities outweigh this, and that any effect is certainly not neutral.

There is a sense amongst some of the members of Catalyst that the Church of Ireland has succumbed to the temptation not to 'rock the boat', and that members of the Church of Ireland are willing to take more leadership than they have been shown on the matter. The effect on the ground is often deemed to be 'silent acceptance in the name of a peaceful situation'. In this regard there is a critical view of the way in which the church has responded to all the issues that have arisen through the crisis at Drumcree. It would appear that at least some parts of Catalyst believe that the church can end up saying something that is so bland and carefully worded that it is almost misleading, or at least gives the impression of a church saying something when in fact it is saying nothing.

Whatever may be the debates within the Church of Ireland, it is illuminating to go beyond this and ask how other members of our local communities view the Order. If one were to ask how others who are not members of the Church of Ireland or the Protestant community look upon the Orange Order, it would help answer the question as to whether a relationship helps or hinders the witness and mission of the Church of Ireland.

There is a definite difference between perception of the Orange Order in urban and rural situations. In rural parts of Northern Ireland it is probable that the Orange Order is viewed more benignly than it would be in larger towns or the city of Belfast. When one asks how the Order is viewed in the country a familiar tale is often quoted. It is the story of Roman Catholic farmers being willing to milk the cows of their Protestant neighbours to enable them to go to Twelfth of July demonstrations. The sentiment behind the telling of the story is that the Order is a simple part of community life, not harming anyone in any way and not regarded in anything less than a positive light by members of other communities. That this may be so in some cases is probably true. There is, no doubt, an attitude of live and let live in many parts of the community, especially where there are no contentious parades. The fact that the ongoing dispute at

Drumcree strains such an attitude is an observation that needs
to be added at this point.

There are other perceptions of the Order voiced by members
of other communities. It is interesting to note the range of perceptions of the Orange Order within the Roman Catholic community, which makes up forty five percent of the community in
Northern Ireland. Perceptions seem to fall into two broad categories within the Roman Catholic community. One section of
opinion may view members of the Order as ordinary decent
Christians, often neighbours, who are part of an organisation
that has a religious, albeit uncritical framework. The point to be
emphasised is that such opinion does exist. There are many instances where the perception is not of Orangemen en mass, but
of neighbours who happen to be members of the Orange Order
at the same time. There is no doubt awareness of the Order's
anti-Catholicism but such has not prevented members being
good neighbours.

Such a benevolent view of the Order is not the total story.
Members of the Orange Order are obviously not the only members of the community who have a particular view of history.
There are members of the Roman Catholic and nationalist community who will have their own reading of history and the role
that the Orange Order has taken in past events. Some in the
Roman Catholic and nationalist community see the Orange
Order as having less to do with religion and being altogether
more political in tone and purpose.

There will be many that will see the Order as a reminder of
the sectarianism that they believe underpinned the formation of
Northern Ireland. In this regard they will see it as an anti-
Catholic organisation that has constantly supported unionism
and that has been part of a right wing unionist establishment in
Northern Ireland. As a profoundly unionist organisation, it is
also seen to be an agent that has been used to block change within
the community structures in Northern Ireland. Such a reading of
history associates the Order with misapplication of the law and
discrimination during vital years in Northern Ireland. A scepti-

cal view of the religious element within Orangeism is to see it as a farce in the sense that this part of it is practised by its membership on one day a year, on the Sunday before the Twelfth of July. Recent parade disputes only serve to reinforce such a perception of the Orange Order. There are many within the Roman Catholic community who see it less as an organisation where the passion is for the gospel, but rather for something much more overtly political in tone and substance. With particular regard to Drumcree and other disputed parades, there will be the sense that it is associated with breaking of the law and other civil disturbance.

Not all members of the Roman Catholic community would regard parades as being a simple celebration of a particular culture. It has to be appreciated that there is a significant section of this community that rather see these events as being associated with marking out territory and assertion of dominance. Their view of many parades is that they disrupt the life of the community and that certain of them have a dynamic surrounding them that has more to do with political pressure than religious and cultural celebration.

The Orange Order is a very visible, and at times loud, expression of a particular grouping. Due to history and perception on all sides, it has become a focus for Catholic resentment. There is a major issue for the Order in the way it is negatively perceived by a large section of the Roman Catholic community, and significant sections of the Protestant community, in Northern Ireland. It becomes an issue for the Church of Ireland when there appears to be an informal relationship between the two. It is inevitable that perception of one will rub off on the other by association. If this were a mere matter of public relations it would not be especially important. However, it is more than that. The Orange Order in its history has shown itself to be anything but a politically neutral or solely religious organisation. Events of recent years in which violence, bloodshed, murder, and paramilitary activity have been associated with the dispute at Drumcree have done much to deeply alienate large sections across all parts of the community. This is a problem that the Institution may or may not choose to see as a priority to be addressed. It is a problem by association for the Church of Ireland.

Appearance can be everything in Northern Ireland. What is it that a Roman Catholic sees when they look at the Church of Ireland and the Orange Order? Do they see a church that in some ways acted as an agent of English conquerors, and that Orange services in some way simply reinforce this? Do they see a church associated with an organisation that has historical and official links with the Unionist Party? Do Catholics regard Williamite celebrations as in some way an insult to their religion, and that association implicates the Church of Ireland? Or perhaps it is that they see neighbours who happen to practice a particular culture and tradition. It will most probably vary with the local situation.

To step outside the detail of this particular situation for a moment prompts an intriguing question. The answer should at least put us on our guard in considering propriety. Is it more politically correct within liberal Protestant circles to be a nationalist? Put in reverse, is it more politically correct not to be a unionist. The cause of unionism has done itself few favours over the years in the presentation of its case. Nevertheless, it is no less valid a political standpoint than nationalism. Whatever fashion may dictate in various circles, fashion is not an argument in and of itself to undermine the legitimacy of unionism as a political thesis. Is it more Christian to be a nationalist than a unionist? It is the author's contention that no political aspiration can claim that it is necessarily most conducive or compatible with authentic Christian living. If, as the author claims, unionism has no more claim of beneficence to the gospel than another, then the same holds true for nationalism. The point of such musing is simple: matters of taste or political correctness are not valid grounds for determining a relationship. The justice and gravity of the situation demands something altogether more substantial.

The position of the clergy
It is interesting to note the caution with which the discussion of

the relationship between the Order and the Church of Ireland is greeted. This caution is most marked amongst those of a Church of Ireland persuasion, and clergy in particular. Within the membership of the Order one is more likely to sense confusion even annoyance that the subject merits discussion at all. There is genuine perplexity as to why an informal relationship that has existed for years should not simply be accepted as the norm. One detects something akin to hurt amongst some when the matter is raised. Hurt can too easily find itself transformed into anger.

Amongst members of the Church of Ireland, especially clergy, who are critical of Orangeism, one detects something that goes beyond caution. What is often unsaid but communicated nevertheless is a view of the subject based on fear. 'Whatever you say, say nothing,' and 'Sure it's only for my time,' are phrases often describing an underlying approach to discussion of this relationship. This is rooted in a belief that if a person says what they really think about the matter they will face a strong negative reaction. At times unspoken is the fear that being honest with a critique of the Order or questioning relationships would mean 'having to pack your bags'. As a consequence of this there is a temptation to keep the peace, as to do otherwise would be to invite conflict.

Many clergy do not view the Orange Order in a critical way and will therefore have no problems in facilitating various services or events. For those clergy who find the issue much more problematic there are many things to influence them in their attitude towards the Order. Let us imagine a scenario in Northern Ireland where a member of the clergy is unhappy with various aspects of the Order and is unwilling to facilitate events.

Rectors are ultimately appointed to parishes by diocesan bishops. To get to that point a bishop meets with a Board of Nomination. This consists of five representatives from a diocese and four elected individuals from a prospective parish. This Board of Nomination, meeting with the bishop, has the task of selecting and nominating a candidate for appointment by the bishop to a parish. The four parochial nominators will conduct the initial process of interviewing candidates. It is by no means unknown for a prospective rector to be asked about his or her attitude to the Order at this point. The author has had experience of this on several occasions some years ago, with a definite sense that a negative attitude would be inauspicious. If a particular parish is attractive to a prospective rector, and a negative attitude towards the Orange Order would seem to materially effect prospects of appointment in an adverse way, there is at least a temptation to be less than frank.

Critical appraisal of the Orange Order, or unwillingness to facilitate services and the like, can provoke strong reaction. Like many other people, Church of Ireland clergy regard their ministry in terms of a personal vocation or calling. It is also a fact that parochial clergy receive their living and a place of abode from their parish. Not only is it a matter of financial welfare but also a case that clergy mostly live amongst their own parochial community. These will be the people that they interact with, not only within the context of parish activities but in many of the other parts of their daily life. In this context one can perhaps have more appreciation for the temptation not to 'rock the boat'.

Clergy are no less in need of the basic means for living than anyone else. Human fear of rejection or anger from their own community is no more attractive for clergy than for others. Clergy are not exclusive in having occupational stress. Whilst not being unique in this regard, many already speak of a sense of isolation or loneliness in terms of social, personal or spiritual contexts. To openly express opinions that may in certain situations only increase this, at the very least gives cause for careful consideration. It is all very well for others who are not in such situations to call for more vigorous response from clergy, and it is certainly easier to suggest that others walk a Way of the Cross that we may never be faced with. Ultimately fear ought not to be the ultimate arbiter in any decision. Yet, pondering the potential consequences suggests an approach that ought to be based on a very solid footing.

A local church is a collection of human beings. A denomination is a larger version of the same. Wherever human beings come together it is unrealistic to imagine that there will be an identical sharing of views on every issue. It is not unreasonable to expect that where a contentious issue arises there may be an open exchange of views on the matter. The way in which a local rector in Northern Ireland may choose to relate to an organisation external to the Church of Ireland, namely the Orange Order, has on occasion been a matter of debate and contention within a parish

Perhaps the language used to describe such disagreement is too clinical. The political atmosphere is fragile at present, and the Protestant community in particular feels quite insecure. In this context any suggestion of change in a local parochial situation to the relationship with the Orange Order may be less than welcome. Let us consider a hypothetical situation in which a local rector decides to change his or her policy regarding the Order. It is not unexpected that such a change may cause debate. It is not necessarily to be expected that a rector's decision in the matter will be universally agreed with. Up to this point there is nothing exceptional. A rector will no doubt prefer that every decision is accepted and supported, but this is not always so in any organisation. However, debate and disagreement can develop into something with more profound implications. Disagreement can become power struggle and a trial of strength. The context of such struggle may be anything from the meeting to arrange an Orange service, a select vestry meeting or greeting a deputation of members of the Orange Order who disagree with a change in local policy.

Where there is unhappiness with changes in the dynamics of a local relationship, it is fair that those who are unhappy should feel that they have a right to express this to a rector and to present their case. In saying this it necessarily follows that those on the opposite side must feel that they have a similar right. What is not legitimate is for such disagreement to become a context for a power struggle between a rector and an organisation that is not only independent of but also external to the Church of Ireland.

There have been occasions when debate in a local context has developed into implied threat if change is made. Perhaps one is not talking of literal physical violence, but a level of hostility and opposition that is considerably more malevolent than a free exchange of views. Were this to be the case in terms of relating to any organisation external to the Church in a local context, it is impossible to see how any such relationship ought to continue.

Power struggles are about particular issues. Yet, behind such struggle can be a profound debate as to future direction and ethos of a church. It can become in certain instances a matter of who *owns* the church. It is obvious that a church is not fundamentally the property of any human being. It belongs to the head of that body, Jesus Christ, and is not the property of any external organisation. For anyone to serve a local church on the condition that it acts in support of his or her organisation is a price altogether too high.

The simple way for any church to determine a relationship with an external body would be to look at its own mission and ethos, consider the ethos and goals of the other body, and determine whether the two are broadly compatible. But, in the context of the history, culture and politics on this island, when it comes to issues such as mission the church cannot be said to have one understanding of the concept that applies right across the board. A lack of clarity about ultimate purpose in the church's mission is something that gets communicated right down to individual parishes. The result is that congregations or church structures are not always as effective as they should be in seeing and identifying the issues that need to be addressed. To raise questions such as the mission of the Church of Ireland, or to ask what impedes or encourages mission, may be seen as theologically admirable but frankly irrelevant to the ongoing life of the parish. Where this is the case there is a danger that important issues are responded to on the basis of pragmatism alone, or worse. It is all too easy to succumb to the temptation 'to leave well enough alone'. Such is only a wise course of action if all is indeed well in the first place.

Each strength has its own potential for weakness. Clear theological direction can give way to rigidity and harshness. A desire not to be dogmatic can lead to vagueness to a point where it becomes impossible to pin anything down theologically. The Church of Ireland has an immediate problem in responding to this issue in that it is not always seen to be strong in thinking through issues in a rigidly clear theological fashion. Perhaps this is due to a desire to be something of a theological middle way or a bridge church. There is also the fact that each parish has such a degree of autonomy. Whatever the case, there is limited mechanism for considering thorny theological issues, especially to the point of resolution.

Tribal chaplains?

There is a temptation for Christian churches in Ireland to regard themselves as having a primary responsibility to be chaplain to their own tribes. Their people will probably be from a similar ethnic, social, cultural and religious group. Needs will not be seen as exclusively spiritual but also cultural. The danger is that areas of need to be attended to extend to the party political. A chaplain to one's own tribe feels a responsibility to voice the needs, hopes and fears of that particular group of people. As the chaplain for one tribe engages thus so chaplains will similarly function for opposing tribes. As this happens so the pressure mounts for the chaplain not to break ranks. In such a role there is no real concept of outreach. It is not so much about mission or applying the teaching of the kingdom of God without fear or favour, as about meeting the pastoral needs of one's own community and representing it. The danger with such an approach is that church becomes perceived, even by its own membership, as being more of a sociological phenomenon than a body of people from diverse backgrounds having one profound thing in common, Jesus Christ as Lord.

If churches primarily function as chaplains to their own tribe there is an almost irresistible force for the demarcation of that church to be on ethnic, historical, social and cultural grounds.

These become the boundaries to define that particular body, and to define it in opposition to others of different background. This is far removed from Paul's declaration that it is allegiance to Christ that gives Christians their most profound identity, and which joins them in relationship to others who may not share similar backgrounds.[83] A desire for universal mission becomes lost in the temptation to define one's church in opposition to others on grounds of ethnicity, culture, and history. Culture is not something to be denied or denigrated. Every one has a sense of their history. Yet there are no sound theological grounds for allowing these to be the key markers of any church. To do so is to embody something unrecognisable in terms of what the New Testament had in mind regarding the identity of the Body of Christ.

Within the context of a church acting as chaplain to its own tribe there are two temptations with regard to the Orange Order. The Church of Ireland has at times strongly supported the cause of unionism. There is also significant overlap of membership between itself and the Orange Order. There is thus a strong temptation to strongly represent the fears and views of its own community, especially with respect to members of the Orange Order. This is all the more so in the context of a divided community. Particularly in the light of Drumcree the other attraction is for the church to keep its head down on the matter, continually kick it into touch, and hope that the issue will somehow go away of its own accord. Neither choice seems to be particularly in keeping with the call of a Christian church.

Any church is called to be something other than a chaplain to its own community. This does not mean, however, that clergy ignore their community, minister to them in a way that is oblivious to their situation, or ultimately treat them as being in some way the enemy. To accept the premise that clergy are not called to be chaplains of their own communities is not to suggest a refusal to pastor them. It is only possible to effectively pastor an individual or group when you have an appreciation for their situation, whilst refusing to patronise them. Pastoral care in any given situation is an attempt to enable a person to make some sort of spiritual sense of their circumstance and to find God's presence in the middle of it all. The motivation for this is that the individual is not only sustained in their situation but also enabled to live in it with a Christian witness that has integrity.

The Church of Ireland needs to approach this issue with a considerable degree of humility. This is not merely born out of a desire to emulate the character of Jesus. It is humility made necessary by the flawed witness of the church in Irish history. As Jesus reminded one group of onlookers, the qualification for being allowed to cast the first stone is to be without sin.[84] Our examination of the church in this regard has suggested a past not without blemish in terms of passion for the gospel or presenting a church identity that is politically blind. There have been times in Irish history when the Church of Ireland has found common cause with the Orange Order. Although at some point the two bodies have begun to diverge, the church has a history that has encouraged the Orange Order and others to perceive it as having been what Ken Kearon describes as something of a 'semi-detached traveller'[85] with the Order.

CHAPTER SEVEN

Concluding the Way Ahead

The Church of Ireland and the Orange Order are entirely separate and autonomous organisations. This is not withstanding the overlapping membership, history and tradition that they may incidentally share. One does not exist for the good of or at the behest of the other. Each organisation must decide what is an appropriate relationship with the other. Whatever historical ties both bodies may have had, the fundamental identity of the Church of Ireland is as a Christian church, with all that that entails. The fundamental essence, ethos and mission of the church must come from the person and character of Jesus Christ. Its most fundamental identity is not to be primarily defined by culture, history or political outlook. In this respect, as a Christian church, it is required to be party politically 'blind' or neutral.

People would often choose not to be in a particular circumstance or to be facing a particularly painful issue. One is reminded of the old anecdote of the tourist who asked directions from a local. 'Sure the way is simple, but if I were you I wouldn't start from here!' Simple advice, but hardly illuminating.

Even on those occasions when a plan of action seems to be clear, we are still dealing with the feelings of human beings. This should not cause a way forward to be tailored to feelings alone, but is a reminder that it is people we are dealing with and not machines.

Pastoral care is not simply a case of being sympathetic or empathetic. As helpful or pleasant as this may be, it is not the sum total of pastoral care in a Christian context. There are times in such care when a prophetic element will be needed if the person is to truly find God's presence in the middle of a situation, or find a way of facing an issue with integrity. We recall that the word prophetic quite literally means to speak God's word into a particular situation. This is not in some sort of generalised way but in a way that is specifically relevant to what is being faced or lived through at the particular time. An interesting exercise would be to read through the gospels and observe the number of times when Jesus spoke into people's lives or to particular situations in a way that brought God's word in a prophetic way. To have a prophetic element in a ministry is not to adopt one particular style or tone. What is important is that God's word is somehow communicated. Jesus spoke in a way that offered people a way of change, but nevertheless did not compromise God's word for individuals or situations.

The challenge for the Church of Ireland with this issue is to pastor a community that feels profoundly insecure. It is to offer something more than sympathy. It is to seek to enable its members to find God's presence in the middle of a historically and culturally complex situation. A necessary element of this pastoral ministry will be the prophetic. One of the vital things about prophetic ministry is that it is hopeful. To speak prophetically is not to compromise on spiritual truth. At times it will be a ministry that brings comfort, at other times it will offer challenge. In general it offers an invitation to a way of living and choices that may not be without pain and cost, but in essence offer a future.

One of the most difficult things to do in a pastoral situation is to offer advice or speak words that one knows will cause pain or offence. Added to this is the possibility that it may also cause controversy. This is no less true when pastoring a community rather than an individual. If anything it will be more pronounced. When offence or hurt is caused there is a basic question to be asked: What is it in the situation that is actually causing the offence? Is the offence caused by what is being said or by the way in which it is being said? With any issue the desire is to present the centrality of the Cross and to apply it to the matter in hand. This may or may not cause offence. Offence should not be given in the way that it is done. There should be no sense that what is being said, or the way in which it is communicated, is being done with arrogance or in a patronising fashion. Applying the principle of the Cross to a given situation requires that those who may take offence have no cause to feel that they are being treated as the enemy or that there is anything less than a complete pastoral commitment to them. It also requires that the issue be addressed with the theological and intellectual rigour that it demands, rather than to depend on one's own personal opinion or prejudice. To seek to do this is not to guarantee that offence will still not be caused. However, beyond this, if offence is given then it is not something that responsibility can be taken for.

One senses from the prophetic ministry of Jesus that his purpose was not to crush, but to offer a different way. In that sense his words were often costly but never unattainable, and essentially life giving. The core of a Christian message in any situation is not only the offer of the Cross, but also the possibility of resurrection into a future. The challenge for the Church of Ireland in this complex matter is in essence to offer the same.

The Cross is not only a potent symbol but also the essence of Christian living. It is not to be confused with suffering for its own sake. For Jesus it was not only the means by which he redeemed the world, it was also the perfect surrender of his will to the Father. To read the gospel accounts of the crucifixion, or observe the struggle that Jesus had in the Garden of Gethsemane as he contemplated what the Cross would involve, is to be left with no illusion as to the cost for Jesus in surrendering his own will to follow that of the Father. The mystery of Christian faith is that, rather than being a place of destruction, the Cross is a means of liberation.

What Jesus offers to any Christian is clear in its simplicity:
If anyone would come after me, he must deny himself and take up his cross and follow me.[87]

The model that Jesus offers for any Christian is essentially the same as the one he followed. The Cross is a place of surrender of one's own will and desires for the sake of whatever the Father's will may be. Whilst there is no illusion that it is a place free of pain or struggle, neither should it be forgotten that it is a place of freedom. Paul describes the pattern of his own life in a description of what walking the Way of the Cross means to him:

> I have been crucified with Christ and I no longer live, but Christ lives in me. The life I live in the body, I live by faith in the Son of God, who loved me and gave himself for me.[88]

The challenge for the Church of Ireland is to present the Way of the Cross to its membership and to those beyond it. In essence it is to search for what it means to be surrendered to God's will in any particular situation. Surrender to God in any given situation rises above pragmatism, history, culture or other competing pressures. There is no suggestion that the matter of the relationship between the Church of Ireland and the Orange Order is anything other than complex. Nor is a desire to be surrendered to God's will necessarily to ignore politics, culture or history. However, it is to refuse to be ultimately defined by it!

In arriving at an appropriate relationship with the Orange Order the Church of Ireland is faced with a challenge. How can it avoid enunciating principles in such a general way that nothing is actually said and no specific issue is addressed in detail or ultimately with any integrity? Yet this is by no means the only challenge. The declaration of various ceasefires in Northern Ireland does not hide the fact that an attitude and atmosphere of conflict exists within the community. How is it possible to address a contentious issue such as this relationship in a way that does not simply increase an atmosphere of intransigence in the community? Is it a contribution to peacebuilding in our community if alienation felt by one group is simply replaced by increasing tension and alienation in another? As a Christian church living in the context of a divided society, the Church of Ireland has a call to act as a peacemaker. Honestly living out this vocation does not exclude a commitment to peacemaking with those who are in the Orange Order. Principle, not mere pragmatism, must guide how such a vocation is to be lived out.

The Church of Ireland has a further dilemma. Many members of the church that are also members of the Orange Order. These are often decent people, good neighbours, not seeking to make party political points or give offence to anyone. For this section of people membership of the Order seems to be motivated by cultural or religious reasons. The public manifestation of such membership is most likely to cause little note or offence, whether or not others share their views. The dilemma lies in the fact that violence, bloodshed, murder and paramilitary activity have accompanied the Orange Order protests at Drumcree in recent years. It has also seen widespread civil disturbance and disruption that is resented by many.

It is the complexity of the issue, combined with the potential consequences of voicing a clear opinion on it, that demands a lead from the Church of Ireland at a church level. Whether on the level of the House of Bishops, General Synod or Standing Committee there is a need for leadership in this matter. It is simply too great for individual clergy or parishioners to work through on their own.

A Sub Committee on Sectarianism, established by the General Synod, highlights some of the issues:

> An act of public worship cannot be entirely divorced from the actions, attitudes and intentions of worshippers before and after the act of worship itself ... There are circumstances in which an act of worship may become the focus for, or the proximate cause of events which give rise to scandal and disorder.[8]

In the same report, the Sub Committee recognised that the issue was in fact wider than the events surrounding Drumcree. It observed that there was a need to look at the wider issue of the relationship between the church and the Order. It observed the existence of a political element to the *raison d'être* of the Order. It is clear that they saw wider issues than the local situation at Drumcree for the Church of Ireland to address. This led it to declare:

The church will have to give mature consideration to the implications of these aspects of Loyal Order parades since the
church will not wish to be seen to be endorsing any particular party political standpoint.[90]

The key issue in all of this is whether or not a relationship
with the Orange Order strengthens or weakens the witness of
the Church of Ireland. The temptation will always be to ask
other questions first, such as what is the pragmatic approach or
what is possible, or simply not to address the issue at all. The
fact that some do not like the relationship being questioned at all
should not decide the matter. Then again, neither should 'embarrassment' or offence to the taste of others.

If there were great doctrinal differences between the two organisations then there could be no question of a relationship.
However, the doctrinal basis for the Orange Order is orthodox
Reformed Christian teaching. In the essentials of doctrine there
seems to be no case to make for a relationship to be inappropriate. The Church of Ireland does not seek dialogue and relationship with other churches on the basis that every detail of doctrinal emphasis will be the same. If this were the case then there
would be little future and less point in ecumenical dialogue. In
broad terms there is little to suggest doctrinal controversy when
asking whether Orangeism stands for beliefs substantially different to those embodied in the Bible, Reformed teaching and
the Thirty Nine Articles.

The Orange Order has a political dimension that is inherent
in its birth, history, and *raison d'être*, and this dimension is clearly
unionist. Party political neutrality is vital if the witness of any
church to have integrity. If an informal relationship exists then
the Church of Ireland must recognise that it is in association
with an organisation that has official links to the Ulster Unionist
Party. It is legitimate for any association of people to want to
maintain the constitutional link with Great Britain, but should
any church be associated or readily identified with this? The
same question applies to nationalism and the propriety of any
church being similarly identified. It would be foolish not to

recognise the interweaving of various denominations in the political history of Ireland, both north and south. It would be wrong to say that members of a church should not be openly involved in political debate or openly be members of political parties. Only the naïve will suggest that the majority of members of the Roman Catholic Church are other than nationalist in aspiration and that a similar proportion of the Church of Ireland are most likely to be unionist. That is not the issue. It is rather to say that it is a step too far for a church to be seen as anything else but neutral in party political terms.

There is much, both on the level of principle and on a practical level, that leaves one unhappy for there to be any sort of relationship between the Church of Ireland and the Orange Order. That this is so is not a matter of taste or preference. Not only have the two organisations drifted apart but there are matters of principle that compromise the position of the church as a politically neutral body, and actions by members of the Order that in recent years have associated the church with violence, civil disorder and murder.

What should the Church of Ireland do? There is always the temptation to leave well enough alone, ignore the issue and hope that it eventually goes away. It is perhaps wishful thinking that events will happily resolve themselves with a minimum of inconvenience to all concerned. Parishes can continue to simply facilitate Orange services but deny any particular association with the Order over and above another organisation. This is all very well and good as long as the same rules apply to all organisations external to the church. An interesting test of this would be the response to a request for a special service or other facility from an independent body less well disposed to the union. The nuances of a claim that facilitating an organisation on an annual basis does not suggest any association may also be lost on the disinterested bystander.

What if the Church of Ireland were to decide that there are such differences of principle and discomfort with the Order that there could be no association? Could the church make a policy decision that there should be a complete break with the Order? If there is no formal relationship with the Order then it is difficult to see in what way such a decision could be enacted. As has already been noted, there is a considerable degree of autonomy and independence enjoyed by rectors and parishes, although the General Synod is the governing body of the Church of Ireland. It is difficult to imagine a realistic mechanism for carrying such a decision into practice.

Transformation

The Church of Ireland has changed. Many of the values and manifestations that gave it the appearance of common cause with the Orange Order are no more. That this has happened over a period of time has disguised the fact that something profound has happened. Whatever the deficiencies of its own history no cause must be given for a belief that the Church of Ireland makes a link between defence of Reformed faith and the maintenance of the constitutional link with the rest of the United Kingdom. A legitimate political opinion is to be argued on its own merits. The link with Great Britain is not a matter of faith within the Church of Ireland nor should it be so.

In any atmosphere of conflict or when dealing with a contentious issue, one desires to act with integrity to principle but also in a way that is not going to add fuel to a fire. Failure to achieve such a balance is likely to result in compromise of truth or an inflaming of tension that makes peacemaking more difficult. Such sentiment finds expression by Joe Liechty and Cecilia Clegg:

> … in the short term it may sometimes be necessary to make decisions or to take actions that have explicitly sectarian outcomes in order, or in the hope that, in the longer term, other choices may become possible.[91]

Arriving at an appropriate relationship between the Church of Ireland and the Orange Order is to seen in the overall context of conflict in Northern Ireland. One of the most pressing issues that any of the denominations faces is how to live out a Christian faith that has integrity but also contributes to peacemaking in this divided community. The great cause and manifestation of this division is sectarianism. The first thing that the Church of Ireland needs to do is to set this particular relationship into the overall context of sectarianism in our community. Having done this it needs to devise and operate long-term strategies that will combat the roots and manifestations of sectarianism.

Sectarianism is not addressed by ignoring it, or by identifying it without devising a way of counteracting it. In identifying sectarianism as a system, Liechty and Clegg comment:

> Most of what is required for the system to continue to flourish is for the majority of ordinary decent citizens to keep colluding in low level sectarianism and subtly reinforcing the divisions between groups ... If we are to be able to move beyond sectarianism it will require active and sustained effort at all levels and in all areas where the system works.[92]

It is clear that there are profound difficulties with the Orange Order that must not be disguised or ignored. It will not help the Church of Ireland to make a useful contribution to defeating sectarianism if the Order becomes either the whipping boy or scapegoat for the church and beyond. It is one relationship that must be addressed. However, if this does not come as part of a wider and more openly sustained strategy to combat sectarianism then it may prove nothing more than a distraction.

An examination of reports and other work undertaken by the General Synod in recent years shows that work on the issue of sectarianism has been done. It is also encouraging to see other initiatives such as the Think Again programme in Down and Dromore Diocese. This is designed to enable parishes to devise strategies for renewal that encompass outreach, young people and reconciliation. If nothing else, the Drumcree issue has highlighted the issue of conflict in our society as an issue for the Church of Ireland to address. Sectarianism is not a fringe issue for the church. It is something that it may learn to live with, and has done so for many years. It is entirely possible for a church in a divided society to carry on with life as normal without a sustained strategy to address this matter. If so, it is done at the cost of a major blight on the its witness.

The Lambeth Conference of Anglican Bishops declared some years ago that the final ten years of the twentieth century should be a decade of evangelism. The fact that it was such an eminent body within the Anglican Communion that had made this call for evangelism meant that it could not be ignored. Evangelism is a concept that many in the Church of Ireland had difficulty with. There was, and is, no common understanding within the church of what was purposed by evangelism or how it ought to be carried out. Nevertheless, the call by the Lambeth Conference placed the issue firmly and publicly on the agenda right across all the dioceses and parishes of the Church of Ireland. By giving such a public lead it made it much easier to have open discussion of the subject and work through its implications. No claim is being made for the effectiveness of any of the programmes that arose from this discussion. The vital thing was that it was publicly placed on the agenda of the church in a way that not only demanded reflection but action. The virtue of approaching the relationship between the Order and the Church of Ireland within a wider context of addressing sectarianism is that a more intelligent and less judgmental response is possible. These issues are too potentially overwhelming to be approached by the individual.

There is a need to provide a strategy that places the broader issue of sectarianism, and the church's relationship with the Orange Order, on the public agenda at a national, diocesan and parish level. The value of such a strategy is not always in the answers that it provides but that it offers a framework whereby otherwise contentious subjects can be openly and legitimately addressed on a local level. Such a considered strategy should be designed in a way that enables people to work through the issues for themselves, but that also faces the members of the church in a non-confrontational truthful way with the simple teachings of Jesus that are pertinent. The challenge is to devise ways in which truths are rigorously applied to present day situations and actions. The overall goal is to allow the teachings of Jesus to speak in a way that ensures members of the Church of Ireland apply unarguable truths in their situation. It is nothing less than a mechanism that has:

> ... an approach of redeeming, transforming and converting people's understanding, attitudes and ultimately the hearts of each person as well as societal institutions, where possible.[93]

Whether it is discussion of the broader issues of sectarianism or the more specific matter of a relationship between the Orange Order and the Church of Ireland, there is a great temptation to deal with immediate manifestations at the expense of long-term roots. The conflict in Ireland has fermented over centuries. If the church is to make an adequate response it will require commitment that is both public and long term. There are practical areas that could usefully be addressed, and which would encourage a lessening of sectarian tension in this matter.

The Protestant community in Northern Ireland is very inarticulate. It is obviously not the case that there is an absence of opinion, but rather that it is not easily verbalised. This does not contribute to a peaceful society, because an inability to articulate and reasonably argue a political view easily leads to frustration, anger and a sense of alienation. If one also accepts the thesis that the Protestant community is both insecure and pessimistic at present, this does not aid its ability to articulate. In the arena of partisan politics, a church must be neutral. It is not the task of a denomination to espouse nationalism or unionism. However, it is a real contribution to peacebuilding if churches can foster political debate and the ability to express a viewpoint in its membership.

Church Services and Parades

One of the more immediate ways in which a relationship between the Church of Ireland and the Orange Order is worked out is in the facilitating of church services. Whatever the context it must be remembered that at all times the Orange Order is in attendance as the guest of a particular church. That this is so is not only recognised by the Church of Ireland but by the Orange

Order in its publication, *Here We Stand*, which sets out its own clear guidelines for the arranging of Orange services.

It should never be the case with any organisation that a church or service is simply handed over to an organisation external to the Church of Ireland. It is the duty of a rector to keep clear control of all aspects of the service, including the preaching of a sermon. The duty in this is to ensure that everything that takes place at such an event is in line with both the teaching and the ethos of the Church of Ireland. Such occasions are often an opportunity for the rector of a parish to preach and address relevant issues of sectarianism and an application of the gospel that is relevant to Christian living in a situation of conflict. Many Orange services are unremarkable affairs and are conducted on the basis already outlined. As often as not they may be arranged through a process of amicable consultation. Were the atmosphere to be otherwise, or a request made on a basis other than that previously noted, there is no case to argue that such a service ought to be facilitated.

Applications for special services or church parades are at the discretion of a local rector. It will be helpful for an incumbent to develop a policy dealing with all such requests by organisations external to the Church of Ireland. This is not an area that falls within the remit of a select vestry. However, it may be useful for informal discussion to take place so that select vestry members are at least aware, and hopefully supportive of such a policy. It seems obvious that any such policy should be devised with the support of the diocesan bishop. The virtue of having something like this in place is that it openly sets the ground rules for all involved. Such a policy should clearly elucidate the fact that it is the responsibility of an incumbent to order services and give permission or otherwise for visiting speakers, all under the authority of the bishop. This is a fact that is already recognised in Orange Order guidelines for the arranging of services.[94]

In considering the request either for a special Orange service or that members might attend a normal service wearing regalia, consideration must be given to the atmosphere of community relationships in an area. If a regular parade has taken place in previous years and has not been the cause or scene of disturbance it will be an unremarkable event. What is to be the case if a parade is associated with violence and civil disorder? In the context of the Church of Ireland's overall mission it is hard to see that such will cause anything other than profound harm to the cause of the gospel if a parade is inextricably linked with a church service. Nor is the Church of Ireland obliged to an agenda that seeks to foster parades disputes for the sake of wider political agitation. That this has been the case on occasion is beyond doubt. Where necessary it is for an incumbent to make a judgement as to whether other agendas are at work amongst those who request or oppose a service, and to act accordingly.

What is quite clear is that the greater interest is in how this involves and associates the Church of Ireland as a church. In this respect it effects the witness of every part and every member of the church, in every place. Whatever is in the minds of the protagonists in this dispute, including the Orange Order, the result is an inflaming of sectarian tension on a national scale. This is a scandal that the Church of Ireland or any Christian church ought not to be associated with or be seen to countenance.

Flags on churches
We ignore symbolism in Northern Ireland at our peril. There is a sense within the unionist and/or Protestant community that whilst the future of Northern Ireland as a part of the United Kingdom was secured by the Good Friday Agreement, there is yet a desire to neutralise public symbols of this. Thus issues such as the flying of the union flag on public buildings, insignia for a new police force, or even the display of certain types of lilies in Stormont become sources of suspicion. It is a cynicism that although the sovereign status of Northern Ireland has been agreed in principle it will nevertheless be gradually undermined by a creeping neutralisation of public symbols to that effect. It is the fear that whilst the struggle has changed on one level, it simply raises its head on others. It may still feel like siege even if the

weapons of war have been replaced by political attrition. As one
unnamed unionist put it when reflecting on the Protestant sense
of siege, 'The siege mentality would go if they would lift the
bloody siege!'

To observe the above is not to deny the fact that other members of the community, whilst preferring another constitutional
arrangement, nevertheless accept the status of Northern Ireland.
In doing so, their agenda is not that as feared by some in the
Protestant community. It is more simply a wish to have symbols
that they can embrace without a sense of alienation. Neither is
our purpose to defend or critique any such fears in the Protestant community. It is simply to observe that they are there.

What has this to do with an appropriate relationship between the Church of Ireland and the Orange Order? Quite a lot
when one considers the importance of symbolism in Northern
Ireland. If such a relationship goes through any process of transformation it will inevitably have public manifestations at various levels of church life from national to parochial. Will some
read into it part of a wider process of neutralising symbolism
with regard to the union with Great Britain?

It needs to be clearly stated and understood that any change
or otherwise in the relationship between the Church of Ireland
and the Orange Order is wholly unrelated to other political fears
or agendas. An appropriate relationship is to be worked out on
solid theological grounds. What also must to be noted is a need
for sensitivity to the fears amongst some in the Protestant community that any change is part of a wider political agenda. It is
not, and should not be so regarded by any part of the community.
Sensitivity is not an excuse for lack of reflection, or paralysis.
Neither ought the reverse to be so.

The 1999 General Synod addressed the issue of the flying of
flags on church buildings. In approaching the issue it recognised
that this practice on occasion caused confusion and controversy.
The full resolution, as reproduced in Appendix 2, was a reminder that the Flag of St Patrick or the Flag of the Anglican
Communion bearing the Compassrose were the only flags

specifically authorised by the church.

It is apparent that flags are flown on some Church of Ireland churches in Northern Ireland at particular times of the year, particularly the months of July and August. The obvious question is to ask why a flag is flown at this time. A commemoration of the Battle of the Somme is one reason that is suggested. This battle and the huge loss of life amongst the Ulster Division is something deep within the psyche of parts of the Ulster Protestant community. It is understandable that such sacrifice and loss of life is remembered. When a flag is flown for this purpose, it will be flown for the actual day of remembrance itself, at the beginning of July.

If flags are not flown for one day on churches, but perhaps for several weeks in July, or indeed all of the summer, it illustrates that something other than the Battle of the Somme is being commemorated. It is obvious that flags are often flown to coincide with Orange Order celebrations. This fact is also highlighted by the fact that it is not only the Union Flag that may be found on some church buildings, but also flags in the colours of the Orange Order. The flying of flags on such occasion sends out a very clear message to church members and to all onlookers. It is an identification of the Church of Ireland with the Orange Order and its celebrations. It is one thing if a local parish chooses to facilitate an Orange service or parade. It is another matter entirely for it to publicly identify with an organisation by the flying of a flag for several weeks or months of the year. The issue is not the flying of the union flag, although it has already been noted that Orange colours are at times flown. It is rather the occasion of doing so. It is quite legitimate for the Orange Order or other lawful organisation to publicly identify and celebrate its culture by all legal means. Unless the Church of Ireland is willing to fly flags to coincide with the celebrations of other organisations it seems to unduly link what are in fact two quite separate bodies.

Given the insecurities present in the Protestant community at present, and the fact that the flying of flags from many church buildings is often regarded as an unremarkable tradition, the matter requires some sensitivity. There are various issues that the church and local select vestries need to feel able to address. Why is a flag flown during particular times of the year? Given that the public celebration of culture within the law is quite reasonable and legitimate, nevertheless why should a church publicly identify with the celebrations of one independent body more than another? What messages are being communicated to church members and onlookers alike when flags are flown in identity with an external organisation? Whatever the affiliations of individual church members, if any church is meant to be officially 'blind', how is it possible to reconcile the flying of flags on such specific occasions?

Ownership of the Church

The Church of Ireland must follow an agenda that is not subject to anything that will deflect it from first priorities. The church is called to express the life of Jesus Christ in tangible ways. However challenging a situation that may be, it is the responsibility of the Church to find a way of living out and prioritising values that are first and foremost to do with those of the Kingdom of God.

A question that every group of Christians has to constantly ask is this: who owns the church? Does church belong to one particular age group, gender, cultural group or political viewpoint? It will be made up of people who represent all of these. It may be the case that particular churches will, by coincidence or otherwise, have a makeup that suggests members that share certain historical, cultural or political backgrounds. Whether or not this is the case, these backgrounds are not to define the most fundamental essence of the church's identity, character or mission. To do otherwise is not only to fall far short of the identity in which church ought to be rooted, it is also to leave church open to being either the servant of or captive to other agendas.

All parts of the Christian Church in Ireland have shown themselves to be far less than politically blind in Irish history. It

is not to criticise Christians for embracing rigorous political debate, having personal party political views or being concerned
for national issues. What becomes the problem is when the body
of Christ in whatever guise seems to become a servant for either
unionism or nationalism rather than the gospel. The danger then
becomes whether or not it is passion for God along with the values of his kingdom, or passion for the nation that has the upper
hand. The Bible is unambiguous about the dangers of supplanting
love for God with something else. It matters not what it is that
may beat passion for Jesus Christ and his gospel into second
place. If the effect is the same then that thing has become an idol,
no matter how finely honed or reverently followed.

No member of a Christian church will suggest that the
church belongs to anyone other than Jesus Christ, its head. The
old saying, 'Possession is nine tenths of the law', may say less
about law but more about the importance of practical reality.
What is on a title deed is not all that is important, but also who in
practice physically occupies the property. The ownership of the
church by its head is not disputed. The clear challenge is for
churches to demonstrate the reality of this in their actions. This
will de facto necessitate a church operating to and working towards its own clear agenda, and only coincidentally to that of
any other external body. The reality of this will be written in the
individual decisions that are made by each parish.

Epilogue

Several years ago I had the privilege of being part of a small team of Christians who went to central Nigeria. A mixed group, our purpose was to lead Renewal Meetings in a particular Anglican diocese based around a large town. Our daily routine involved travelling from our accommodation in the suburbs of the town to a venue in the centre, and back again. Inevitably one left refreshed in the morning and made the return journey perhaps in more jaded mood after a series of meetings during the day. On most days this journey was unremarkable.

On one particular Friday we set out for a return journey having led various meetings. It soon became obvious that town was much more crowded than usual. This seemed to be due to the fact that a large number of men had spilled out onto the streets. The crowds were so large that groups of men were quite simply sitting in the middle of the streets. These people were quite orderly and not especially menacing in intent. What had on previous days been a straightforward journey became much more tortuous as our driver constantly diverted to try and find roads that were not blocked by these great crowds of people. It mattered not that these people seemed to have no particular intent. The result for us, as well as anyone else travelling that day, was considerable inconvenience and diversion. Whether it was the heat, tiredness or the prospect of a meal being delayed, my mood steadily worsened as the journey wore on. It became positively indignant when I was told that this was a regular occurrence every Friday. The area we were in was evenly divided between

Christian and Muslim. Our hosts informed us that the crowds of men were Muslims who had just finished Friday Prayers and were now spilling out of their Mosques onto the public thoroughfare. It seemed as though they were simply taking over the streets.

I could contain my indignation no longer. How, I wondered aloud, do you put up with this every week? How dare these people put others to great inconvenience on a regular basis? My musings were added to in a most unexpected way. 'That is just how I feel at home,' remarked one of our team. This person happened to be a Roman Catholic from a small and unremarkable town in Northern Ireland. At a loss to know what on earth this remark meant, I listened as they explained how they felt that their freedom was curtailed by a large number of Orange Order parades and band parades that took place in the town each year. When these took place they felt as though they were put to great inconvenience on a regular basis, and that on occasion the atmosphere was quite menacing. What was being communicated was a sense of loss of ownership of one's own town.

Indignation did not turn to understanding on my part. Irritation and then anger was rather the result. I had got on well with this member of the team. A feeling of exasperation born out of incomprehension overwhelmed me. It seemed just typical to me that we had travelled three thousand miles, were involved in stimulating ministry, and yet just couldn't leave Northern Ireland politics at home for three weeks. How was it possible to equate the inconvenience on these hot dusty streets with events in Northern Ireland? How unfair to equate this seemingly outrageous inconvenience with Orange parades. It was anger that grew out of a feeling that this person had spoilt the atmosphere with a wholly inappropriate and unwarranted comparison. The party had been spoiled and I knew who was to blame. The trouble with anger and irritation is that it does not always go away by itself. A good lunch and a rest did not do the trick and we were soon on our way back to lead further meetings, with my anger still smouldering.

Who knows what causes the proverbial penny to drop in any given situation? It was not any rigorous line of thought on my part, or a sudden overwhelming desire to see the other person's point of view. In the middle of a meeting I began to slowly understand what my colleague had been trying to say. I looked back on my own feelings of outrage, inconvenience and a sense that the crowds were somehow claiming ownership of the streets, whatever their intentions might have been. As someone who by background is not instinctively threatened by Orange parades, I got a vivid glimpse of what a person from another tradition might experience.

It is uncomfortable to find ourselves in the other person's shoes. It is a place that few of us travel to willingly. Even were we to willingly travel down such a road, it is hard truly to feel the reality of another person's experience. This is all the more true when that person resides on the other side of the fence. The desire to express our own sense of outrage, grievance and insecurity seems so urgent and overwhelming that there is simply no energy to begin to imagine how the other person might feel. The communities in Northern Ireland each have their own weight of history, outrage and injury bearing down upon them. Where do our feet stand today? Who would we name as the person or community from whom we feel alienated or simply regard with incomprehension? Even a fleeting experience of what it may be like to stand in the shoes of the other is as revealing as it is startling. It does not negate the need to make decisions of principle, but nevertheless holds out the possibility of renewing a right spirit within us.

However, more than a right spirit is needed! As essential as it is to put ourselves in the footsteps of another, it still does not answer the core question. What is the appropriate relationship between the Church of Ireland and the Orange Order? The major temptation for much of the Church of Ireland is to attempt to muddle through the issue. The form this sometimes takes is to ignore it for fifty weeks of the year and to effectively relinquish control of the church for two weeks in July, all the while putting pangs of unease to the back of the mind. The source of unease may come from a sense that our approach may have more to do with expediency than principle. The substantive issues of difficulty previously outlined make this an unworthy response, as does the immediate scandal of Drumcree.

The Orange Order is a profoundly political organisation. This is a statement of objective fact rather than opinion. Not every member of the Order is profoundly political in outlook, though some are. Not every Orange demonstration is a noticeably political event, but undoubtedly some are. The Order has shown itself to be political in its actions since the signing of the Good Friday Agreement as it has expressed an anti-agreement stance. This may make it no more or less political than an organisation expressing a pro-agreement view. We have already noted the political stance of the Order that is easily traced through the development of the Unionist Party and beyond. However, none of this provides the most fundamental grounds for asserting the essential political nature of the organisation. It is not merely political in its historical actions. If that were to be the definitive criterion, then most churches in Ireland could be defined as profoundly political. It is the intimate binding of evangelical Protestantism with the defence of the union that makes it political in its very substance. Its most fundamental theology is the linking of anti-Romanism, a version of unionism and the defence of biblical faith. This is what makes it political in its very essence. To take away this is to leave something that would not be recognisable in any sense as Orangeism.

Whatever the deficiencies of its history in terms of party political neutrality, the Church of Ireland is in its very essence a body whose profound allegiance is to Jesus Christ and to the living out of his gospel. As a Christian church it cannot add a political philosophy to this or define its mission in terms of one. We state again that unionism is a legitimate political aspiration. The Church of Ireland has been at times something of a co-traveller with the Orange Order in the cause of unionism. It is undeniable that many members of the church are unionist in outlook. This ought not to be a source of embarrassment or defensiveness within the Church of Ireland. Active and intelligent political engagement of all peaceful types should be encouraged amongst the membership of any church.

Drumcree is relevant not just as an issue of the moment but as a symptom of wider and deeper struggles within our community. The Church of Ireland has become trapped and is being used in the Drumcree situation. This is something that it should not tolerate. As the situation has been played out, a realisation has dawned among many members of the Church of Ireland and the Orange Order. It may appear ironic given the situation. Difficult to articulate it is nevertheless profound. Put simply it is the realisation that the Church of Ireland is no longer part of the party political voice of unionism or a co-traveller with the Orange Order in its cause.

The fact that the Church of Ireland ought no longer to be there to articulate the cause of Orangeism, or any other party political stance, is slowly becoming obvious to more and more members of both the church and the Order. This may be a cause of resentment and anger to some who will feel that yet another 'voice' for the broader unionist community has been lost. In itself it is part of the broader soul searching that needs to take place within the unionist and/or Protestant community – essentially that unionism is a valid political philosophy in and of itself. It can and ought to stand on its own merits without theological justification. It does not need the imprimatur of any denomination. This is liberating both for the political stance and for the denomination. The same is also true for nationalism.

The Church of Ireland has a number of options when considering an appropriate relationship with the Orange Order. It can pretend that difficulties already alluded to do not exist. This carries with it the realisation that difficulties do exist but a blind eye is turned at certain times of the year. Such an approach offers the line of least resistance. It may seem pragmatic, but is dishonest not only to itself but also to members of the Orange Order. It leaves open the accusation that there is an abdication of control of the church for at least parts of the year. Previously cited matters of concern and the immediacy of Drumcree force the issue out into the arena of open discussion.

A further option would be to suggest a total and sudden break with the Order. This would be manifest in the refusal to facilitate Orange services or any other such events. Pristine theology is always easier when not confronted with reality. Such an approach would have two effects. There are many members of the Order who are decent law abiding citizens and honourable members of their church. Members of an organisation with a profound political emphasis they may be, but the effects of such a sudden break on would be traumatic to say the least. Into this context comes the insecurity that the Protestant community in Northern Ireland feels at present. Apart from the trauma of a sudden break, it may also fuel the more extreme elements of Orangeism in a way that greatly increases the atmosphere of sectarianism.

The appropriate relationship between the Church of Ireland and the Orange Order is one of progressive disengagement. It lies somewhere between turning a theological blind eye and action that may inflame more sectarian tension. It ought not to be a subversive or hidden course of action. It begins with the unequivocal public understanding that the Church of Ireland, whatever its history, is no longer necessarily a fellow traveller with Orangeism. The working out of any relationship at local level should be done within clear guidelines that are there for all to see. Any sign that the Order, as an external body, has undue influence over a local parish or that the facilitating of already existing events is damaging to local Christian witness or community relations, suggests a relationship that is locally inappropriate.

Orangeism is synonymous with unionism. The cause of unionism has become politically incorrect in liberal circles, the reverse being the case for nationalism. A process of disengagement should not be taken as a criticism of unionism any more than it is an espousal of nationalism. It takes place within the context of a unionist community that combines insecurity with a difficulty in articulating itself. It will doubtless be seen as abandonment and betrayal by some. However, unionism, like nationalism, needs to come of age. It needs to realise that it is a political belief that stands on its own merits. The theological rationale that Orangeism gives is less and less relevant in liberal democracies at the beginning of the twenty-first century. It is one with which Church of Ireland cannot identify.

The key fact to be noted is that the Church of Ireland and the Orange Order have moved from a place where they once had much common cause. It is now much more clearly seen that they are separate bodies independent of one another. A process of transformation is not as clear-cut as some may wish. It does not come with the quick answer that may be desired. Northern Ireland is paying the cost of the consequences of such 'solutions'. It will be a step too far for others. Yet to do less is to cast principle aside for the sake of pragmatism or fear.

The Church of Ireland has truth to bear witness to. It is not lived out in a sterile vacuum but in the messiness of real life in Northern Ireland. It must be at liberty to articulate truth that is not captive to any party political philosophy or grouping, and that is spoken without fear or favour. A process of disengagement is what is already becoming apparent to many both within the church and the Order. It takes place in the context of a politically insecure unionist population. To disengage must never be an excuse to demonise. Parity of esteem extends also to the Orange Order.

APPENDIX 1

Sample Policy re Requests for Special Church Services or Church Parades

1. Requests for special church services or church parades may be facilitated where such a request falls into one or more of the following categories:
- If the request is from, and for the sole benefit of, a parish organisation.
- If the request is for a service or parade that is already a traditional and/or annual event in the parish calendar.

2. In accordance with the Church of Ireland any such decisions are for the rector to make.

3. The ordering of such services is by the rector, in consultation with those requesting a service.

4. The rector will preach at all such services.

Guidelines for Arranging Orange Services
Taken from Orange Order Publication *Here We Stand*

The Loyal Orange Institution, with a membership drawn from the great majority of the Protestant churches, is an rrganisation fully pledged to the upholding of the Reformed faith. Naturally therefore we seek to enjoy good relationships with the evangelical communions. These relations can be maintained and nurtured if we for our part are careful to observe the courtesies which should always prevail in such relations.

In organising anniversary and other services the following should be observed:

- When the use of a church building is envisaged, it is only proper to approach the Minister-in-Charge of the church in good time, to request permission for its use. This is always advisable even where a service has been traditionally associated with one particular building.

- If a special preacher is desired then the permission of the Minister-in-Charge of the church must be given before any invitation is issued to the preacher. All the denominations have their own rules regarding the control of the pulpit. These rules must be respected and the local incumbent's permission given before a visitor can occupy his pulpit. In many cases the local pastor may wish to issue the invitation to the special preacher personally and this must be respected. It is therefore better not to make any approaches to a guest preacher until the matter has been cleared with the local Minister. If a suggested name is not acceptable to the local Minister there can be no question of the decision being disputed.

- The conduct of the service is also a matter for the Minister. This includes the order of service as well as the hymns, prayers, collections etc. These must all be acceptable to the Minister-in-Charge, whose conscience, as well as his position in law, must be respected at all times. It is therefore of great importance that those who are organising such services should consult with the Minister-in-Charge about all these items, well in advance of the planned event.

- The colours recognised by our Institution, the National Flag and the Standards of our Religious Order are often carried into church. When this is done they should be borne in a dignified manner. Here again local sensitivities should be consulted. Some Ministers may wish the colours to be brought in at a point in the service where they feel that it is most appropriate. While good order in carrying and presenting the colours is of course highly desirable, it should be remembered that we are not a military organisation, nor is our regalia the equivalent of military uniform. The colour party, being male, should therefore remove headgear before entering the church building.

In the majority of instances no difficulty arises. In a small number of cases where a problem may exist, courtesy and awareness of sensitivities should obviate unnecessary offence.

General Synod Report 1999
Standing Committee Report: Appendix Four: Resolution 1

The General Synod of the Church of Ireland recognises that from time to time confusion and controversy have attended the flying of flags on church buildings or within the grounds of church buildings. This Synod therefore resolves that the only flags specifically authorised to be flown on church buildings or within the church grounds of the Church of Ireland are the cross of St Patrick or, alternatively, the flag of the Anglican Communion bearing the emblem of the Compassrose. Such flags are authorised to be flown only on Holy Days and during the Octaves of Christmas, Easter, the Ascension of Our Lord and Pentecost, and on any other such day as may be recognised locally as the dedication Day of the particular church building. Any other flag flown at any other time is not specifically authorised by the Church.

Bibliography

Acheson, A., *A History of the Church of Ireland 1691-1996*, Columba Press, Dublin, 1997.

Bingham, W., *Making Sense of Northern Ireland*, Grand Orange Lodge of Ireland, Belfast, 1997.

Boal, F. W., Keane, M. C., Livingston, D. N., *Them and Us*, Queens University, Belfast, 1997.

Bowen, D., *History and the Shaping of Irish Protestantism*, Peter Lang, New York, 1995.

Brewer, Higgins, *Anti-Catholicism in Northern Ireland 1688 –1998*.

Brokeness, Forgiveness, Healing and Peace in Northern Ireland, Lectures in St Anne's Cathedral, 1996.

Brown, T., *The Whole Protestant Community: The Making of a Historical Myth*, Field Day Theatre Company, Derry, 1985.

Bryson, L., McCartney, C., *Clashing Symbols*, Institute of Irish Studies, Queens University, Belfast, 1994.

Buckley, A. D., *Symbols in Northern Ireland*, Institute of Irish Studies, Queens University, Belfast, 1998.

Chittick, G., *The Enniskillen Men*, Grand Orange Lodge of Ireland, Education Committee, Belfast.

Dewar, M. W., *Why Orangeism?* 1987

Dewar, M. W., Brown, J., Long, S. E., *Orangeism: A New Historical Appreciation*, Grand Orange Lodge of Ireland, Belfast, 1967.

Dudley-Edwards, R., *The Faithful Tribe*, Harper Collins, London, 1999.

Dunn, S., Morgan, V., *Protestant Alienation in Northern Ireland*, Centre for the Study of Conflict, University of Ulster, 1994.

Church of Ireland Gazette, 28 July 2000, 22 September 2000, 9 February 2001

Church of Ireland Journal of the General Synod 1999.

Cusack, J., McDonald, H., *UVF*, Poolbeg, Dublin, 2000.

Elliot, M., *The Catholics of Ulster*, The Penguin Press, London, 2000.

English, R., Walker, G., *Unionism in Modern Ireland*, Macmillan Press, London, 1996.

'Guidelines for Arranging Orange Services' from Orange Order Publication, *Here We Stand*.

Hall, M., *Beyond the Fife and Drum*, Island Publications, Newtownabbey.

Hempton, D., *Religion and Political Culture in Britain and Ireland*, Cambridge University Press, Cambridge, 1996.

History of the Royal Arch Purple Order, Research Group to Enquire into the origin, purpose and development of the Royal Arch Purple Order, 1990.

Jarman, N., *Material Conflicts: Parades and Visual Displays in Northern Ireland*, Berg, Oxford, 1997.

Jarman, N., Bryan, D., Caleyron, N., de Rosa, C., *Politics in Public Democratic Dialogue*, Belfast, 1998.

Kennedy, W. A., *Celebration 1690–1990: The Orange Institution*.

Kirkpatrick, C., *The Glorious Revolution*, Grand Orange Lodge of Ireland, Education Committee, Belfast.

Liechty, J., *Roots of Sectarianism in Ireland*, Belfast, 1993.

Liechty, J., Clegg, C., *Moving Beyond Sectarianism*, Columba Press, Dublin, 2001.

Long, S. E., 'The Influence of the Orange Institution and the Interaction of Other Movements in Protestantism and Unionism in Northern Ireland, 1921–1989', Thesis for Geneva Theological College, Mermill, 1990.

MacCarthy, R. B., *Ancient and Modern: A Short History of the Church of Ireland*, Four Courts Press, Dublin, 1995.

Malcolson, W. A., 'An Expose of the Royal Arch Purple Order' (Taken from: *Behind Closed Doors*).

McDonald, H., *Trimble*, Bloomsbury, London, 2000.

McGarry, J., O'Leary, B., *Explaining Northern Ireland*, Blackwell, Oxford, 1995.

McKittrick, D., *Through the Minefield*, Blackstaff Press, Belfast, 1999.

Meridith, I., Kennaway, B., *The Orange Order: An Evangelical Perspective*, 1993.

Milne, K., *The Church of Ireland: A History*, Universities Press, Belfast.

Montgomery, G., Whitten, J. R., *The Order on Parade*, Grand Orange Lodge of Ireland, Education Committee, Belfast, 1995.

Montgomery, G., *The Orange Institution in Ireland*, New Ireland Group, Open Meeting, Ulster People's College, 1997.

Nelson, S., *Ulster's Uncertain Defenders*, Appletree Press, Belfast, 1984.

Open Letter to Christians in the Loyal Institutions, ECONI, Belfast.

Press Release from the Rector and Select Vestry of Drumcree Parish, 18 September 2000, The Church of Ireland Press Office, Belfast.

Ross, M. M., *Orange Order: What it Stands For*, Strule Press, Omagh, 1964.

Ryder, C., *Shades of Orange*, Cultural Traditions Group, Belfast.

Sibbett, R. M., *Orangeism in Ireland and Throughout the Empire*. Vol 1, Thynne & Co, London.

Storey, E., 'Assess the Development of the Psychology of Unionism and its Particular Challenges as the Future Beckons', Dissertation (un-published) completed for M Phil, Irish School of Ecumenics, 1998.

Stewart, A. T. Q., *The Narrow Ground*, Gregg Revivals, Aldershot, 1989.

The Formation of the Orange Order 1795–1798, Grand Orange Lodge of Ireland, Belfast, 1994.

Walker, B., *1641, 1689, 1690 and All That: The Unionist sense of History*, Irish Review, 1992.

What is the Orange Order? Grand Orange Lodge of Ireland, Education Committee, Belfast, 1997.

Whyte, John, *Interpreting Northern Ireland*, Clarendon Press, Oxford, 1998.

Williams, T. D. (ed), *Secret Societies in Ireland*, Gill and Macmillan, Dublin, 1973.

Wilson, M. (ed), *The Future of the Orange Order*, Conference Report, Belfast, 1995.

Advisory Group

Clarke, Rt Rev K.	Bishop of Kilmore Diocese
Kearon, Dr K.	Director of the Irish School of Ecumenics, Dublin
Kennaway, Rev B.	Presbyterian Minister. Member of Orange Order. Former member of Grand Orange Lodge of Ireland Education Committee

Notes

1. Evangelical Contribution on Northern Ireland
2. Matthew 28:19-20, Acts 1
3. Luke 10:25-37
4. p. 195
5. Ross (1964)
6. p.128
7. Stewart (1977) p. 15
8. Stewart p. 16
9. Jackson (1992) cited in Walker (1996) p. 71
10. Wright (1996) p. 1
11. Dudley-Edwards (1999) p. 128
12. Walker (1992) p. 64
13. Stewart (1989) p. 167
14. Jarman (1997) p. 67
15. Dewar (1987) p. 8
16. Dewar (1987) p. 22
17. R Quigley interview 18.8.00
18. Patsy McGarry interview 19.10.00
19. What is the Orange Order? p. 3
20. What is the Orange Order? p. 5
21. Rev G. Sproule interview 7.6.00
22. What is the Orange Order? p. 3
23. Dickinson (1997) p. 4
24. Boal (1997) p. 110
25. Gordon Lucy interview 6.6.00
26. Jarman (1997) p. 56
27. Dudley-Edwards (1999) p. 32
28. Twelfth July Demonstration 1998
29. D. Chillingworth interview 8.8.00
30. McDonald (2000) p. 85
31. Dean Griffin interview 22.6.00
32. John Dickinson interview 11.04.00
33. McGarry et al (1995) p. 212
34. p. 20
35. 1999 General Synod Report p. 140

36. Galatians 3:26-28, NIV, Hodder and Stoughton, London, 1989
37. Luke 10:27
38. Luke 10:28
39. p. 175
40. Archbishop Temple
41. Matthew 28:19
42. Acts 1:8
43. Charles Kenny interview 16.6.00
44. Book of Common Prayer p. 335
45. Alan Acheson interview 10.4.00
46. David Quinn interview
47. McCarthy (1995) p. 11
48. Orange Lodge Publication, *Here we Stand*
49. Liechty (1993) p. 4
50. Milne p. 23
51. Elliot (2000) p. 70
52. 'From theologies in opposition toward a theology-of-interdependence', *Life & Peace Review*, vol iv (1990) p. 13
53. Elliot p. 167
54. Elliot p. 167
55. Liechty (1993) p. 21
56. Dr Duncan Morrow interview 2.4.00
57. McCarthy (1995) p. 54
58. Interview 8.8.00
59. Quoted in *What is the Orange Order?* p. 3
60. GOLI
61. Dr E. Culbertson interview
62. Liechty & Clegg (2001) p. 103
63. Liechty & Clegg (2001) p. 114
64. Alan Falconer, World Council of Churches
65. Duncan Morrow interview 2.4.00
66. Liechty & Clegg (2001) p. 115
67. Matthew 19:16-24
68. David Quinn interview
69. 1 Corinthians 9:19-22 (NIV)
70. Luke 10:25-37
71. Luke 10:28
72. Luke 10:29
73. Luke 6:27-28
74. 1 Kings 18:25
75. Ruth Dudley-Edwards interview 4.10.00
76. *What is the Orange Order?* p. 2
77. *Steadfast for Faith and Freedom*, Education Committee of the Orange Order, Belfast, 1995, p. 3
78. Bruce (1986) p. 265
79. Bruce (1986) p. 247

80. Denis Murray
81. Friday 28 July 2000
82. Liechty & Clegg (2001) p. 140
83. Galatians 3:26-28
84. John 8:2-11
85. Ken Kearon interview January 2000
86. Matthew 26:26-42
87. Matthew 16:24
88. Galatians 2:20
89. Sub Committee on Sectarianism Report 1999 p. 173
90. Sub Committee on Sectarianism Report 1999 p. 173
91. Liechty & Clegg (2001) p. 106
92. Liechty & Clegg (2001) p. 109
93. Liechty & Clegg (2001) p. 121
94. See Appendix 1 (Sample Policy on Parade and Service Requests)